THE CATS OF AMERICA:

How Cool Cats and Bad-Ass Kitties Won The Nation's Heart

Séamus Mullarkey

The Cats of America:

How Cool Cats and Bad-Ass Kitties Won The Nation's Heart

SPECIAL BONUS!

Want This Bonus Book for free?

Get FREE, unlimited access to it and all of my new books by joining the Fan Base!

SCAN W/ YOUR CAMERA TO JOIN!

Dedication

This book is dedicated to my niece Éabha Slattery and her special visiting cat friend Guggen Annie. It is also a most fond tribute to my mother, the late Kathleen Mullarkey, who loved books more than anything and passed that relentless drive to read to her own children and to her many pupils. She was also known to microwave milk for stray cats on frosty Irish mornings, for which the feline world owes her a debt of gratitude.

Acknowledgments

Thanks to all those friends and family who were so encouraging about writing yet another chapter in the big, wide world of cats. I'd like to offer a word of gratitude for my past employer and literary mentor, the late Helen F. Pratt. She emphasized that a book about any topic under the sun could be worthwhile, just as long as it was interesting and well-written. I like to think she would enjoy this literary offering. Finally, a special thanks to Sharry for her talent and insight...

Preface

America has had quite a complex historical connection with its kitty companions. Over the centuries, they've been a great part of all our major developments, from the railroads and postal service to television and even space travel! From spoiled couch monsters to bedraggled street cats, from hard working kitties to brave-hearted little lions, they've all played a role.

Although haughty and indifferent at times, America's cats have been known to show compassion and bravery towards their furry neighbors as well as their adopted two-legged friends. It only makes sense for us to give back by building them grander cat towers, providing them with fancier kibble cuisine and higher quality care. As we look toward the future, I'm pretty sure the American people will always have those intrepid furballs scampering alongside us.

Happy reading!

Séamus Mullarkey, November 2021

CONTENTS

Introduction

A merica is a land that has captured many people's imaginations, both those who live here and those who may only experience it through books or movies. It's a land made up of many kinds of people, a significant number of whom, despite widely differing interests and temperaments, all would consider themselves "cat people." In its relatively short history, this country has seen huge movements of people, astounding technological advancements, and wave after wave of commercial ingenuity and social reinvention. But how could any of this have been possible without the help of our feline friends?

When pioneers chopped wood to build cabins in the west, there was little Tiger chasing rats around, keeping the fermenting cheese safe from scavengers. When a rural housewife left an apple pie burning in the oven, the incessant mews of Madame Kitty notified her of the impending fire in her bakery. When the Wright Brothers created the first airplanes, they had no idea it would lead to thousands of flights taking off every day filled with anxious folks jammed together 30,000 feet in the air. Did they also come up with a way to calm these people? No, but our furry friends come to the rescue yet again! Tucked away in her designer carrier is a reassuring cat companion, the feline emotional support specialist, soothing rattled nerves with every purr.

Snuggling at our feet and curled up into furry bundles, our kitties sleep with contentment, knowing how much they do for us every day. But have we any idea how much of an impact they've had on this great nation as a whole? Warm up some milk for you and your tiny friend, for it is cocktail hour. Join me as I take you through a dazzling tour of kitty trivia, tantalizing tales, and meow-gical adventures...

Gotta Love That American Spirit!

Workin' Hard

The All-American work ethic has always defined America. Although cats are languid and somewhat lazy creatures at first glance, the nation has also known many felines who were prepared to put their whiskers to the grindstone.

In 1895, the *New York Times* reported the breeding of thick-coated "refrigerator cats" in Pittsburgh who were specially trained to hunt rodents in cold warehouses. These refrigerated warehouses radically changed America's eating habits, allowing for all kinds of food to be transported and stored, including plenty of seafood—even many hundreds of miles away from the coast. The long-lost breed of albino longhairs who patrolled the frosty perimeters of the storage spaces was said to even *purr-fur* sleeping on frozen pipes in a room already kept at a harsh 10 degrees Fahrenheit! We hope they were rewarded with some tasty chilled tidbits from among the stock of frozen foodstuffs. A lobster popsicle for a diligent kitty, perhaps?

Equally as important as the distribution of food is the supply of books to a nation of ravenous bookworms. To that end, it's worth noting the story of two hard-working Scottish Fold cats, Baker and Taylor (named after the largest book distributor in the world). These official employees of Douglas County Library in Minden, Nevada were originally "hired" by the librarian in 1983 to help with a persistent mouse problem, but the library would add more duties to the kitties' job description, such as the courteous greeting of patrons, guarding of office supplies (by sleeping on them), and customer service at the checkout station. News of these new hires would reach Baker & Taylor, who made the kitties their official company mascots! Posters of these employees of the month would go on to decorate the walls of libraries across the country.

Elsewhere, the Mount Washington Observatory has had a record of employing four-legged weather crew dating as far back as 1930. They even compiled a work log noting all the names of these feline co-workers. Amongst many, many names of furry employees are included the tailless Tikky, Oompha—mother of five, timid Elmer, and Inga the calico. These cats bore the heavy responsibility of warming the laps of observers during the mountain's cold winters and providing inspiration for souvenir merchandising by modeling for t-shirts.

These fine felines have shown that any hard-working kitty can certainly make it in this country. I'm sure you'll agree they're an inspiration to us all. Now, I wish you good luck as you try to get your own fluffy freeloader to roll off the La-z-Boy and get a job…

Anyone Can be Purr-sident

Quite a few of America's leaders have been cat lovers, starting with the founding fathers. Now, while Thomas Jefferson is said to have liked cats, he didn't bring a cat with him to the White House. However, he did bring a mockingbird who would entertain visitors by making meowing sounds! The very first official felines to set foot in the White House were Abraham Lincoln's kitties, Tabby and Dixie. It was no secret how much this president loved these furry friends. When asked if her husband had any hobbies, his First Lady simply replied, "Cats." Yet, for Lincoln, cats and their care were not just a hobby but rather a constant preoccupation. Once, when the Civil War was ending, Lincoln was on his way to General Grant's headquarters when he spotted three small kittens freezing in a telegraph hut. After learning that their mother had died, Lincoln took them into his arms and brought them home to stay in the White House until furr-ever homes could be found for them.

It must be noted that Lincoln didn't keep his cats out of sight in domestic quarters. They were on the same level as any visiting dignitary and accordingly granted respectful hospitality. It was said that the First Lady once informed Lincoln of her embarrassment when he fed his hungry kitty with some valuable ceremonial dining implements during a formal White House dinner. He responded, "If the gold fork was good enough for former President James Buchanan, I think it is good enough for Tabby." Yes, Mr. President, a point very well made!

Many more cat lovers would come to be Commander-in-Chief, from Rutherford Hayes and his pair of Siamese to William McKinley and his two Angoras. Then, there was Woodrow Wilson. He owned cats named Mittens and Puffins, who had to be squirted with water to stop them leaping on the dining table during family meals. Bad kitties! Calvin Coolidge was a cat lover from an early age, and he once saved a litter of kittens from being drowned. While in the White House, his feline retinue consisted of the cats Bounder, Mud, Blacky, Timmie, and Tiger. Coolidge liked to hide Bounder around the White House. The First Lady once found him inside a hall clock. And on Sundays, boisterous Bounder got to ride down the laundry chute, something he apparently loved a great deal. Timmie, on the other hand, was so gentle, he often slept with a presidential canary named Caruso, perched on his back or nestled between his paws.

Coolidge's beloved Tiger, however, would cause quite a public commotion. He once traveled a half-mile away to the Navy building and stayed there for a few days, worrying the president so much that he put out an earnest appeal for his return using that relatively new means of communication, the radio. The next morning, the guards found the wandering kitty and returned him to the White House. Upon his return, Tiger was outfitted with a collar identifying him as a resident of the White House. However, the restless feline wandered away a second time and, alas, this time, did not return.

Teddy Roosevelt had a gray, six-toed kit named Slippers, who liked to disappear and reappear wherever he pleased. On the evening of one state banquet, Slippers was obliviously sprawled out in the middle of the hall carpet. As Roosevelt walked down the hall, an ambassador's wife on his arm, he noticed the cat and simply bowed to him, then led the woman around the furry detour before continuing without missing a beat. The procession of well-dressed dignitaries behind Roosevelt followed his lead and walked around Slippers, who was too busy napping to even notice the inconvenience he was causing to Washington's diplomatic elite!

In more recent times, the Kennedys owned Tom Kitten, who was considered important enough to receive an obituary in a Washington newspaper, being honored as part of the magic that was Camelot. In the 1970s, the Fords owned a sealpoint Siamese, named Shan Shein after a city in China, while the Carters owned another Siamese named Misty Malarky Ying Yang (as someone whose surname is 'Mullarkey' I feel her pain...) The Reagans didn't bring cats with them to the White House but did keep some kitties at their ranch. Presumably, those felines shied away from the Washington spotlight, and who can blame them? I wouldn't want to feature on the evening news every time I clawed an armchair… Chelsea Clinton's cat Socks was one of the more prominent presidential pets of recent times, with the president referring to her as Chief Executive Cat. He even walked her around the White House grounds on a leash! Given this kitty's obvious importance to the president, it's hardly surprising that she had her own page on the White House website. George W. Bush had a trio of much-loved kitties while in office. India "Willie" Bush was a striking black cat named after Texas Rangers baseball star Ruben "El Indio" Sierra. Another kitty, Ernie, was named in honor of Ernest Hemingway, but (echoing the turbulent restlessness of his namesake) turned out to be too much of a free spirit for the stifling confines of an official residence. He was dismissed from his high office and sent to live with out-of-state friends. However, sources say that President Bush's most beloved kitty was Cowboy, who sadly died of kidney disease shortly after the president started his term.

Dreaming Big

Many of us in America dream of making it big one day. Get-rich-quick titles top the bestseller lists and images of billionaire lifestyles dominate social media feeds. Cherry Pop, the fabulous red Persian, is one feline who turned that dream into a reality. She was the prized pet of Vi and Huey Vanek, millionaires from Fort Lauderdale, Florida. In the late 80s, Cherry Pop flew to shows across the country, completely sweeping championships and taking home the top prizes. Talk about being the cat's meow…

When Cherry Pop visited San Francisco, the Mayor actually gave her the key to the city! In Los Angeles, she met with such high-profile fans as Doris Day, Betty White, and Angie Dickinson. She was even crowned Queen of the City in Boston. Me-ow, what a glamourpuss! Cherry Pop's residence included an aviary and a garden full of squirrels located outside her favorite picture window, for her viewing pleasure alone. She dined on choice lean steak, Evian water, and skim milk.

That pampered Persian wasn't the only feline to have experienced the high life. In the 1960s, a certain Doctor Grier left his cats, Brownie and Hell Cat over $400,000. What about the meek? It seems that instead it's the furry who will inherit the Earth. I am seriously considering buying a catsuit and finding some billionaires to adopt me. Come on, folks, what have I got to lose?

The Ultimate Consumer Society

Commerce made America powerful, but it has been advertising that oiled the wheels of commerce, communicating with a mass audience, alerting them to deals and steals, and boosting their desire to try the latest and greatest. This medium of purr-suasion has played a vital role in American society, and it's only logical that our fine felines would have played their part. If you thought Don Draper of the TV smash *Mad Men* was the cat's meow of the advertising world, you probably aren't aware of the long history of American's feline purr-suadors. As early as 1889, cats started showing up in ads across America, like the little black kitty on the bottle of Black Cat whiskey. Now, production of that liquor did end abruptly due to the prohibition of the 1920s, but a black cat would go on to star in several other successful campaigns, such as the catchily named Snappy Snap dresses during World War I.

One of the most highly advertised products of the 19th and 20th centuries was tobacco. That is, it was until most US advertising and promotion relating to it was banned. Quite a few brands of cigars and cigarettes had feline links, such as Black Cat cigarettes. I'm glad that the whole shameful business of cats promoting tobacco was eventually put to rest in the 1980s with several cat-themed commercials from the American Lung Association, urging people not to smoke.

In 1933, not long after the construction of their railroad, the Chesapeake and Ohio Railroad selected an endearing mascot, a tiny sleepy kitty named Chessie, whom they promoted on the cover of *Fortune* magazine with the slogan, "Sleep like a kitten on the C&O." It didn't take long for Chessie to become a national treasure with her own line of clothing, jewelry, calendars, and even pocket knives! I guess not all of us have sharp claws to get ourselves out of tricky situations…

Another sensation of the 1930s and 1940s was Snowy, the fluffy white spokescat for Utica and Mohawk Cotton Mills. She would be featured in magazines such as *Woman's World* as she went out shopping for soft cotton sheets, laundered them, ironed them, and finally, used them to make a bed the *purr*-oper way!

One especially lucky ad-cat was found at the humane society by animal trainer Bob Martwick just before he was scheduled to be euthanized. That orange tabby would later be named Morris and had his debut role as the 9 Lives cat food spokeskitty. Morris became the most notable feline in the advertising industry and went on to star in the film *Shamus* (as someone named Seamus, I'm dying to watch that one!). It stars Burt Reynolds and Dyan Cannon. Morris then "wrote" three books about pet health, care, and adoption, was featured on the covers of *Good Mousekeeping* and *Cat Fancy: 30th Anniversary* and stamped his paw print on a bill at the White House. When he happily retired, many other kitties would audition to play the next Morris. Ah, Morris, that's life as an American success story, always someone younger and furrier, nipping at your tail, waiting for their shot at the big time...

If such stories intrigue you, you might like to track down a copy of *The Cat Made Me Buy It!* It recounts multiple stories of cats who promoted products and was authored by advertising manager Alice Muncaster and humane director Ellen Yanow. With over 100 colorful illustrations, it's a treat to purr-use.

Playing A Key Part in Our History

Native Americans and Their Sacred Cats

In the 1980s, the remains of a young animal were discovered by archaeologists in a burial ground near the Illinois River where Native Americans of the Hopewell Culture had resided approximately two thousand years ago. At the time the remains were labeled as being those of a puppy as the Hopewell did commonly bury their dogs with them. However, decades later, evolutionary anthropologist Angela Perri opened the box and realized immediately that the find had been misidentified. Her instinct was that it was a cat of some kind. Further study revealed that it was a bobcat (*Lynx rufus*) who was only several months old. Amazingly, the bobkitten wore a carefully crafted necklace made of bear teeth and shells.

Photographs of the excavation seem to indicate that the bobcat was intentionally buried with some reverence, as its paws were deliberately placed together. While researchers are unsure whether Native Americans commonly domesticated bobcats or if this was an isolated incident, it's clear that this bobkitten was considered a special animal. Its necklace and careful placement in the burial mound would seem to indicate that it was. Could this be the first pet kitty we know of within what is now the United States?

Artifacts show how prevalent wild cats have been in Native American culture, represented as they were in old drawings as well as by headdresses made from wild cats' skulls. For instance, warriors would paint their faces with whiskers and claws. After European settlement, when *Felis catus* (the good ole house cat to you and me) was introduced, these domesticated felines found a place for themselves among Native Americans much as they had already done among Europeans, partly as rodent control, partly as pets. Some interesting photographs from the early days of photography show Comanche people on horseback with cats perched on their shoulders, although whether this was just an anomaly is hard to ascertain.

Land Ahoy!

When Christopher Columbus first sighted the Americas, his first thought was of what part cats would play in the continent's future development. Hmm…Well, as a cat lover, I'd love to think this was true, but it would just be a big, fat, old, furry fib on my part to make such a claim. However, the first domestic cats here did make land from European ships where they had been employed as pest control and as companions on those long, wind-tossed journeys. Some were brought on board intentionally, while others snuck onto ships. Whether these stowaways did so in search of overseas adventure or simply in hot pursuit of a plump, tasty rat without thought of where that pursuit might eventually lead is unknown to recorded history. We doubt they came in search of cities of gold, although if those legendary places included palaces full of overstuffed velvet cushions, that could have been a purr-suasive factor! Whether these kitties who arrived in America yearned for the cozy fires or snug barns of their old countries or immediately took to their new home is a matter open to speculation. Such conjecture might be a suitable topic for an amusing work of fiction. Let me know if you'd like to read such a volume, and I'll see if I could write something worthy of your interest…

Mayflower Kitty—The Original and The Re-Enactor

Mrs. Heaney was a passenger on the Mayflower in 1620. History doesn't grant her the same status as some others. You may never have heard of her, but she played a very important role in the history of American feline history. Her family Bible proudly recorded that her cat gave birth on Plymouth Rock shortly after the ship landed, a fact brought to light by her descendent and cat breeder Kay McQuillen. That historic mama cat must have been quite relieved that those little furballs arrived safely on dry land. Talk about losing no time in making oneself at home in a new country! The descendants of the "first founding cat" found useful occupation in their new domain. Interestingly, their pest control duties were not just limited to houses and barns. They patrolled the open fields as well. William Wood's book *New England's Prospect* observes that squirrels plagued the precious corn crop until fed-up farmers released cats among the plants to fight off the pesky varmints. Can't you just see groups of cats chasing squirrels with gusto, and doubtless being praised and petted mightily for doing so?

In 1955, a replica of the Mayflower was built and sailed from Britain to Plymouth, Massachusetts. Project Mayflower was conceived to commemorate military cooperation between Great Britain and the United States during WWII and to pay homage to the two countries' intertwined heritage. The re-enactment was given a special feline touch by a diminutive, black-and-white kitten named Felix. Some of the crew had misgivings about bringing this teeny, little youngster on the voyage. After all, the boat was a faithful replica of the original and had none of the comforts of a modern vessel. Life aboard would be tough indeed.

Well, this intrepid kitty proved them all wrong! Whenever the ship rocked, Felix clung onto the ropes with the grace of an Olympic gymnast. When bunks were soaked from the weather, he always managed to find the driest spot on the ship. The only injury he ever faced was a broken leg from accidentally being stepped on—the curse of a tiny ball of fluff on a ship full of heavy boots! However, his injury mended in record time, and Felix resumed his onboard routine.

When the Mayflower replica successfully landed in America, Felix joined the crew in their celebratory parade and even scratched the presiding Mayor's hand! You can't take some cats anywhere, can you, whether to the vet or to a whole new country? Due to quarantine laws, it wasn't practical for Felix to return to England, so he quickly settled into his welcoming Boston home. Despite his voyage to America having been just a facsimile of the original, this kitty found his new life in America to be the real deal and, by all reports, went on to live a long and much-indulged life.

Witch Hunts

In the sixteenth and seventeenth centuries, the persecution of witches in Europe reached a fever pitch, with up to 80,000 suspected unfortunates put to death during this time. Sadly, European settlers brought their witch hunts with them to the shores of America. The Salem Witch Trials were perhaps one of the most prominent examples in US history. No cats were recorded as being harmed during those trials, which was noteworthy as it was a common belief that witches used cats as assistants (or familiars) for magic spells and could even transform into felines themselves. Unfortunately, two dogs were executed, and for that, all pet lovers of any ilk will surely bow their heads in sorrow.

Still, some American witch hunts did feature cats. The Witch of Pungo, Virginia, Grace Sherwood, was accused of transforming into a cat and damaging crops. It's said that after her death, her sons laid her body near a fireplace, and it vanished into mid-air! Unnatural storms soon followed, as well as a spate of loitering black cats around her home. Frightened farmers set out to kill all the cats they could find, which ultimately resulted in an infestation of rats that destroyed crops in Princess Anne County, Virginia, in 1743. And they said *she and the cats* were the ones damaging the harvest? In recent years, actions have been taken to acknowledge and mitigate, in some small way, the wrongs that were done to Grace Sherwood. That poor beleaguered woman was granted an unofficial state pardon in 2006 to restore her good name, and a statue remembering her was erected in 2007. The sculpture shows her in the company of a raccoon (as she loved all animals) and carrying a basket of rosemary, which represents her knowledge of herbal healing, presumably an endeavor that would have aroused suspicion as plant remedies were closely associated with witchcraft. To all present-day American cat lovers who dabble with herbal salves, and pride themselves on the healthy state of their oregano, be grateful you do not live in times where such innocent pursuits might lead to persecution.

Holding the Fort in Savannah

During the Civil War, a fearless, black feline by the name of Tom Cat was much loved by the Fort McAllister garrison in the Confederate city of Savannah, Georgia. He would zip along the defenses, dodging the crossfire of musket shots and cannonballs during battle. You'd think that would make him as nervous as a cat on a porch full of rocking chairs (as they'd say in the South), but there was something spectacularly brave about this kitty. The lucky cat was on his ninth life when he was eventually struck by a stray bullet during a naval assault from the Union forces. He would be the only casualty at the fort that day.

With heavy hearts, the soldiers buried Tom Cat and held him a service with full military honors. The reports of his death-in-action were even mentioned in official military correspondence to General Beauregard, who was defending Charleston from similar naval attacks at the time.

Today, visitors, staff, and war re-enactors at Fort McAllister frequently report seeing glimpses of a black cat darting between rooms and sitting outside overlooking the lake. Despite staff affirming there are no cats residing at the fort, visitors often feel the soft touch of fur brushing along their legs, only to look down and see nothing there. It seems that even 150 years later, Tom Cat is still holding the fort...

Westward Meow!

In the early 1800s, European settlers headed west to explore the frontier and establish new territory. The first courageous cats to accompany them would do so in a wagon train, a series of horse-drawn wagons in a line as long as the modern-day diesel train. Imagine your fluffy kitties pulled by horses. I can just see my spoiled cat enjoying this. Well, that is, until the roads start getting bumpy and wet with rain.

There are a few intriguing accounts of settlers and their cats. For instance, there are some notable mentions in the much-loved works of Laura Ingalls Wilder. In "Little House in the Big Woods," she recounts leaving behind her first cat, Black Susan, in Wisconsin, where the kitty continued to live in the little house that they abandoned, which had been turned into a corn crib. Poor Laura, she must have missed her kitty so! Black Susan presumably stayed to protect the stored corn from those who might seek to munch on it throughout the colder months when it was sorely needed for food by the farmers.

This was not to be the only important cat in Laura's life. In Chapter Three of "Little Town on The Prairie," entitled "The Necessary Cat," she tells of her father soundly sleeping in his bed, only to awake to find a fearless mouse chewing off his hair to build a nest. Yikes! The family immediately sought to put the rascally mice in their place by acquiring a recently-born kitten whose eyes were not even open. Pa Ingalls thought that the little mite was too young to be separated from its mother, but as cats were in short supply in the Dakota Territory, he paid the princely sum of fifty cents and took it home with him. Later called Kitty, the feisty feline grew up to be capable of taking on even the fiercest dogs around.

It seems Laura's family got a bargain. There are reports from the 1880s stating that at times the average value of a cat had soared to $10, equivalent to over half a pioneer's average monthly income. Savvy entrepreneurs in the Midwest made a pretty decent living by purchasing cats in bulk and shipping them to the Dakotas by railcar to be sold for an eye-watering profit. Meanwhile, in Gold Rush Alaska, cats were literally "like gold dust," as miners paid for their expert exterminators using that powdered commodity . Nowadays, even though many of our darlings weren't paid for with precious metals, we're sure they're priceless nonetheless!

At The Heart of Our Great
American Institutions

Lounging Around Our Libraries

The first public library in the USA was founded in 1731 by Benjamin Franklin. It was called "The Library Company of Philadelphia," bringing knowledge to the common people who otherwise had no access to it. No wonder such lending libraries were referred to as "the poor man's university." Books were so much more expensive than they are for the modern consumer. Back then, some volumes cost about the same as what a laboring family (both parents earning) might make in a week. Imagine the excitement then when one could access many books hitherto out of reach. Libraries continue to offer a wealth of information to all and a great source for cat books, too! It only makes sense that kitties should have their place in these hallowed halls... Although, given that these are scholarly spaces, only the gentlest of purrs and the quietest of mews should be permitted.

There has been quite a deal of attention focused on library cats in recent years. It's estimated that there are approximately 800 worldwide. You may be aware of the best-selling book "Dewey the Library Cat." It's well worth the read if you have the time. However, my personal favorite among the library cat stories is that of Herbie, who was a chubby tabby and assistant librarian at the Herbert Hoover Presidential Library of Iowa. The tale begins back in 1979 when Herbie showed up at the library steps soaking wet, shivering, and starving for some spare kibble. The doors of the presidential library opened to let him in, and the rest is history. It wouldn't take long for Herbie to truly become the feline president of the library, supplied with a gazebo food dish and his own sleeping cottage, a replica of President Hoover's childhood home.

Greeting over 150,000 tourists a year, furry President Herbie was sure to put a smile on the face of every one of his constituents.

Elsewhere in the US, the Glendale Central Library is home to the world's largest collection of cat books and goods. From feline fiction, history, and breeding reading material to *purrfect* antiques and kitty tarot cards, the amount of para-*furr*-nalia to paw through is endless! The collection was originally founded by librarian Barbara Boyd, who gathered over twenty-thousand publications and items, mostly through donations from the Jewel City Cat Club.

The Library Cat Society was founded in 1987, and it recognizes over three dozen libraries that employ their own feline workforce. All of this is in accordance with US labor laws, of course. Their founder, Phyllis Lahti, would encounter her first library cat, a black and white tabby comfortably stretched out over a window perch at the Rome Public Library in Michigan. She would later rescue the blizzard-trapped stray named Reggie to employ as the first feline at her home library in Minnesota. With over fifteen thousand libraries nationwide, the society works to promote the welfare of these library kitties and support their role as ambassadors, who communicate the need to respect and care for our furry friends to all whom they encounter.

The U.S. Postal Kitties

When the United States Constitution was ratified in 1789, The Postal Clause was written to give congress the power to establish post offices around the nation. America later took a very important step in feline history when it put aside money in the federal budget for hiring cats to control the mouse populations in postal offices. $1,000 was divided and allocated to cities every year in proportion to the amount of mail they processed. We're certainly glad the legislature took this important step. Can you imagine the damage caused if rodents had been left free to chew through pay checks or important documents sent by mail! Oops, those pesky mailroom mice ate the deeds to my house. Again…

As well as a physical presence in post offices, cats have also allowed their likenesses to enliven our correspondence in the form of feline-themed postage stamps. Charles Lindbergh, an American aviator who became the first person to fly across the Atlantic Ocean in 1927, considered bringing his cat Patsy along for the trip. While she ended up not joining him in flight, the little black kit did join him as the very first feline to appear on an official government stamp! However, it was not an American stamp but a Spanish one, which touchingly depicted a forlorn fuzzball gazing longingly at the sky as his daddy flew over the horizon. Thank you, Spain, for doing what the United States ought to have done. It wasn't until decades later, in 1972, that the US issued its first cat stamp, featuring a black cat on a shop counter, commemorating 100 years of ordering products by mail. The first full issue of a series of cat stamps was released in 1988. This release happened came on the heels of an issue of dog stamps, which had prompted a public outcry from some cat lovers demanding that felines be granted a similar honor. Ah yes, those cat people! They're he most *fur-midable* of activists! The four-stamp series included an American Shorthair portrayed with a Persian, a Maine Coon paired with a Burmese, an Abyssian alongside a Himalayan, and a Siamese depicted with an Exotic Shorthair. More recently, 2002 saw an adorable kitten gracing a stamp that advocated for spay and neuter, a most worthy of causes.

Starting in 1897, about 30% of New York City's mail traveled through an intricate pneumatic tube system. Those who operated it were called "Rocketeers." Connecting twenty-two post offices between Manhattan and Brooklyn, packages were launched at 30 mph to reach a quarter of a mile in a minute and a half. During the opening ceremony of the tube system, a demonstration featured the launching of an artificial peach inside a mail canister. When this delivery was successfully received, more items would follow, such as a Bible wrapped in the American flag, a copy of the US Constitution, and, rather strangely, a tortoiseshell feline carried in a cotton sack...

In his 1931 autobiography, postal worker Howard Wallace Connelly wrote that he was amazed that the cat survived moving through the tubes at such a high speed, making several turns, before reaching his destination. After coming out dazed and confused for a minute, the cat recovered quickly and returned to normal behavior. This cat would not be the last animal to travel via these postal tubes. Another cat in need would be transported this way to a veterinary office, as well as dogs, monkeys, and even a goldfish, until the official closure of the system during World War I. The postal service would then transition to a more cost-efficient system, one more familiar to all of us, the automobile, while continuing with the pneumatic system in a much-reduced capacity, until 1953, when the system was finally consigned to history.

Fighting Fur Their Country

A country's infrastructure is never more vital than during wartime when food supplies are essential for a nation's survival. It should be no surprise then to learn that our feline friends were regularly deployed to barracks, ships, and military locations during times of conflict. Here they played an essential role in protecting food stores and preventing the spread of disease, as well as keeping wires and machinery secure from gnawing by pests.

During World War I, the United States launched a Cats for Europe campaign in which they shipped special units of military kitties to help the European allies who were lacking such furry soldiers. It's estimated that half a million felines were drafted into the trenches of Europe during the war.

Fast forward to World War II, when Captain Midnight, a black cat from Dallas, Texas, was shipped to Britain, where it was intended for him to be flown on an RAF bomber that would cross the path of Hitler's advancing armies, presumably to bring bad luck to the Axis forces. The *New York Times* headline of August 2, 1941, indicated that he flew in a red, white, and blue crate labeled "special envoy." Meanwhile, back home, cats employed by the military were even allowed a ration of powdered milk, a commodity that was in scarce supply even among humans at the time.

Rules and Regulations

Have you ever looked at your cat and wondered if you could list him or her as a dependent on your tax forms? With the amount our kitties eat every day, they surely should be considered as such…? It's worth noting that in the 1980s, a deaf man claimed that the cost of caring for his cat should be a tax deduction. He made the case that his ever-alert kitty was always ready to alert him to danger if he couldn't sense a nearby threat, thereby acting as a hearing aid for him, and was thus classifiable as a medical expense. The IRS approved his claim and stated that in the future they would examine any similar situations on a case-by-case basis to determine their validity. Now, I'm keeping a journal to record every possible way I could use my cats as a tax deduction. Maybe you should consider doing the same? Let me know how it pans out…

Moving away from the more mundane subject of tax regulations, I'd like to focus your attention on some more arcane areas of feline law. Apparently, in Sterling, Colorado, the law books state that cats must wear a taillight when running outside at night. I wonder if this was a typo, and they meant to say *cars*, not cats. Could be… Meanwhile, in Cresskill, New Jersey, cats are required to wear three bells on their collar to properly warn birds of their whereabouts. This makes sense to us, for as fluffy and harmless as our darling cats might seem to us, they can pose a significant danger to certain dwindling bird species.

On a somewhat sillier note, in Barber, North Carolina, cats and dogs are not allowed to fight, while cats are strictly forbidden from consuming beer in Natchez, Mississippi. That's all right I'd say, as most of our distinguished, high-class cats probably prefer wine… In California, felines are banned from publicly mating within 1,500 feet of a school, tavern, or place of worship. With my serious hat on, ridiculous as it is, I could maybe see why such a law might exist for a school or church, but why a tavern? Is this related to the cats drinking beer legislation in Natchez? Answers on a postcard, please…

All goofiness aside, we've also had some meaningful laws passed to promote the wellbeing of our sweet kitties. In 1973, President Ronald Reagan (then governor of California) signed a bill into state law that would send a person to prison for kicking or injuring a cat! That was definitely a step in the right direction for animal welfare.

Crime Don't Pay!

Kitty Crimes and Misdemeanors

Before you start worrying that you're misplacing things, you might want to keep an eye out for a sly cat-burglar. In 2003, Simi Valley, California, was taken aback by the criminal antics of a four-legged pirate, a feline by the stealthy-sounding name of Midnight. This klepto kitty roamed far and wide in search of purr-ecious booty. Some of Midnight's favorite items to steal ranged from shoes to hats and even undergarments… Oh my! One Christmas, he even came home with a nicely wrapped present. Midnight wouldn't wait for Santa Claws; he was determined to get what he wanted when he wanted it! Remind you of anyone that you know?

Common career advice holds that one should specialize and establish a narrowly defined area of expertise. Carve out a niche for yourself, they say. Well, that's exactly what one criminally-minded kitty did in Pelham, New York, back in 2006. You see, a white and gray kitty named Willy became especially skilled at slipping away with gloves and nothing else… It got to the point that his human, Jeanine Goche, erected a large sign over her home announcing that a feline glove snatcher resided there. In front of her house, the sheepish pet parent placed a clothesline on which the stolen gloves hung. Ms. Goche hoped that in this way their proper owners might reclaim them. We despair of such criminality among our feline friends and sincerely hope that you are not unwittingly housing a criminal mastermind. Who knows, it might be time for a serious kitty heart-to-heart about the dangers of a life of wrong-doing, just to be on the safe side?

Claw Enforcement

Human nature being as flawed as it is, we'll always have lawbreakers in our midst. So, we'll continue to need police cats to catch them. Yes, you read that correctly… In case you didn't realize it, upstanding felines have been playing a part in law enforcement for quite some time now. These skillful crime stoppers have been in action from way back as mousers and as mascots. For instance, in the 1930s there was a feline who was exceptional in his pest control duties. We're speaking of none other than a black cat called "Homicide." Yes, quite a fitting name for a police cat, we're sure you'll agree! This fella meant serious business. In 1934, he strolled right into the Manhattan Police Headquarters and snatched himself a job catching rats! Homicide would carry them in his mouth and drop them onto Lieutenant Smith's desk blotter, giving his superior a nod before returning to his stationed watch in the basement. The Lieutenant was quoted as saying, "I've seen them come and go in my time, but never before a cat that brings 'em back alive and books 'em. I'm recommending a citation for an extra ration of liver."

Speaking of New York City police cats, recent feline members of the force have also made their mark. I'm thinking of Fred, NYC'S very own undercover kitty. He came to prominence in 2006 when he was part of a sting operation to catch someone posing as a vet without proper licensing or training. The mission was successful, and as a mark of respect, he received a Law Enforcement Appreciation Award from the Brooklyn district attorney and the Mayor's Alliance Award. Unfortunately, poor dear Fred was killed soon after in a road traffic accident, yet we're sure his crime-fighting spirit lives on.

The Boston Police Department has even had a cat mascot for their SWAT team. It's not that surprising, really, considering kitties are remarkably good at *swatting*. The orange calico came to the station as a young stray in 2013 but quickly showed how much of an asset she was to the team. She has provided much-needed stress relief for a unit that must be prepared to handle any deadly situation at the drop of a pen. Just the presence of this feline officer helps to maintain a healthy workplace environment for the whole department. She sure came a long way for a cat from the streets and now resides in a specially built cat condo, complete with a spacious deck suitable for alfresco dining. Talk about landing on your (four) feet. Have you seen the price of Massachusetts real estate recently?

A Stranger's Just a Friend You Haven't Met

Looking Out for Your Fellow Man

Newspaper and magazine archives are replete with accounts of felines in heroic acts of self-sacrifice, from attacking armed criminals to dashing into burning buildings on rescue missions. When you gaze at your lazy ones grooming their fur, do you wonder about the brave undertakings they have the potential to make? We all purr-ay that we never have to witness these moves in action, but if there ever does come such a day, rest assured that it just might be within their feline capacity to protect or rescue us. Here are just a few examples of such kitty heroism…

Saved by a Phone Call

In January 2006 the Columbus, Ohio police received a phone call with no one on the other line. "State your emergency," the police operator prompted. But there was only silence… The operator hung up and tried redialing the residence. Unfortunately, there was no answer. So, the home address was traced, and officers were dispatched to the location immediately.

Upon arriving, police would find Gary Rosheisen, a wheelchair-bound man, fallen onto the ground. Suffering from osteoporosis and mini-strokes, Rosheisen was unable to dial his phone. He wasn't wearing his medical alert necklace, and he couldn't reach the paramedic-alert rope in his room either.

Rosheisen's orange kitty, Tommy, however, was found sitting next to the telephone. The calm, even-tempered cat was adopted by his owner three years prior to help lower his blood pressure and keep him company. In those three years, Rosheisen also used his free time to teach his cat how to press the speed dial on his phone for 911. He told reporters that he was unsure if the training even worked since they never had to actually speed dial 911 until that eventful day.

Well, if anyone ever doubted the true intelligence and heart-warming care that a feline could have for their human companion, those misconceptions should be shooed out the window faster than a cat chasing a mouse! Rosheisen says that his dear cat saved his life by simply pressing the pre-designated number on the phone. "He's my hero," he declared. And, who could disagree?

Scarlett and her Kittens

In 1996, a massive fire blazed through a New York City garage. Amongst the flames that the firefighters fought hard to put out, they spotted a small litter of kittens that couldn't have been more than four weeks old. That's when the momma cat was spotted, a badly burned stray calico pacing back and forth between the fiery garage and the street outside, where two small kittens mewed for her attention. This dutiful mother was charging in and out of the fire to save each of her babies, enduring traumatic injuries along the way.

Fortunately, a keen fireman, an officer Giannilli quickly realized the situation and helped momma cat rescue the rest of her kittens. Faster, Fireman Giannilli! Momma needs help! While recovering at the vet afterward, the scrawny street cat would be given the name Scarlett after the crimson burns that now marred her calico fur. News of Scarlett's heroism was beamed across the globe, with callers as far as Cairo and Japan reaching out to the shelter with offers of help.

Scarlett's surviving kittens would quickly be adopted into loving homes, and the brave lion-heart found solace with her new Brooklyn family. Although the tips of her ears were amputated and her vision was impaired by smoke damage, her physical and emotional scars would heal. I think you'll agree that she earned the right to be pampered for the rest of her life.

Feline Foils Kidnapper

One San Diego kitty by the name of Samantha was devoted to her neighborhood pal, a little girl named Jennifer. Every day, the little gray cat would greet Jennifer on the sidewalk as she walked home from school. Well, that is, until one day when the feline waited as usual, only for the girl not to come by. Samantha meowed to alert her owner, Charlie Jones, who also found it strange that Jennifer had gone to school in the morning but hadn't returned home yet.

Being a retired cop, Jones decided to drive to the girl's parents to check on her safety, the kitty riding along with him, of course. Upon arriving, he would discover that the parents had just reported their daughter as having been abducted. The police were at that moment on their way to apprehend her kidnapper. Jones hopped back into his car and raced over to act as backup.

At the scene, Jennifer was being clutched by her kidnapper in one hand while he held a weapon in the other. He ordered the police to back away immediately, or else the by-now terrified child would be harmed. Just a few moments later, however, the intrepid feline Samantha took matters into her own claws by leaping on the kidnapper's back. She clung onto him, fangs buried deep into his neck, whereupon he dropped his weapon and struggled to tear the determined kitty off him. Police moved in to bring Jennifer to safety and arrest her abductor. Thankfully, this particular crime story had a happy ending. There's a lesson to be learned here. Don't ever cross a cat, especially if they're looking out for their best friend. You'll be sorry you did…

Kindness Towards Other Creatures

It's in a cat's nature to offer protection, companionship, and some soothing nurturing. You've probably observed that this kinship can be felt amongst feline friends and also between felines and humans. It should be no surprise, then, that cats are capable of building remarkable connections with other species in the animal kingdom.

Momma Cats

One phenomenal mother of seven, Fluffy of Argos Corner, Delaware, took in an additional five babies to care for after their mother passed away. And even more surprisingly, these adopted babies were actually squirrels! It doesn't matter that these kids were buck-toothed nutcrackers, this momma cat loved them all the same.

Another maternal cat Missy unfortunately birthed two ill kittens who would soon pass away. She cried as she searched the home for her babies. It wasn't long until Missy went outside and found herself some new "kittens." Missy's owner watched her carry in four white bunnies by mouth, nestling them into her bed and encouraging them to nurse on her belly.

This was unusual behavior for any cat who might normally hunt small critters. However, it seems Missy really thought these were her babies! Eventually, the bunnies would be returned to their rabbit mother, who quickly moved them to a different neighborhood. After all, mother rabbit was only doing as most mothers probably would if someone stole their babies…

Baby Cats

Zoo World in Palm City Beach, Florida was the home of Tondayelo, an orangutan who became severely depressed after losing her mate. Poor old Tonda lost interest in playing, eating, or doing anything besides laying around by herself. This all changed when a one-year-old orange tabby cat came along, who was very demanding of Tonda's attention. Tonda quickly became close with the little bit of fluff, carrying him around like a baby, feeding him, and even bringing him under the blanket whenever it was time to nap together. The tabby would be named TK, short for "Tonda's Kitty."

This remarkable story is not the only instance of a captive primate bonding with a cat. In 1984 Koko the gorilla was taught American sign language by Stanford University's Dr. Patterson. Around her twelfth birthday, Koko signed to her trainer that she wanted a cat. From a litter of abandoned kittens, Koko picked out a small, gray Manx and named him "All Ball." The two took to each other like mother and son up until the day that All Ball passed away. For days afterwards, Koko signed the words "sad" and "cry" as she mourned her feline companion. Sigh, many of us know all too well how that feels…

Always on The Move

A Vast and Restless Land

It's easy to forget how big the US is. There are some interesting maps online comparing it to other nations, but one of the most thought-provoking for me was an overlay diagram showing that thirty (that's right, three-zero) European countries could be shoe-horned inside the USA. This immense expanse means there's lots of space to move around, and the average American relocates over 11 times during his or her lifetime. That's a lot of cat carriers on the move at any one time! Reasons given for this national willingness to relocate range include the fact the whole country has a common tongue. For instance, you don't have to learn a new language to move from Michigan to North Carolina. In addition, (for better or for worse) greater ease of hiring and firing than elsewhere means job opportunities can spring up in some areas as they decline elsewhere. So, we (and our kitties) have got a lot of moving around to do. Thankfully, technological and infrastructure advances have made this process consistently more convenient over time. As working from home grows in popularity, more and more folks will have their kitties as company during their professional lives as well as during their downtime. They say WFH will allow many people to move away from high-priced locales to places where housing is cheaper. The result might be more money to spend on cat habitats and organic catnip. Let the kitties know the good news, won't you? We're sure they'll be pleased...

Hitting the Rails

The first inter-state railroad for commercial movement of people and goods was chartered for construction in 1830 to run from Baltimore, Maryland, to Ohio. This endeavor allowed passengers to travel around the country more speedily and for shipping of purchases to happen far more rapidly. This massive technological development would bring much prosperity and change to the nation, and it's only right that our feline comrades get their paws on such an important part of *hiss*-tory.

Other railroads would then be built at a rapid pace, involving backbreaking labor on the part of many diligent workers and the accumulation of vast fortunes on the part of some savvy investors. The completion of the Transcontinental Railroad in 1869 captured the public's imagination. Soon, dashing adventures of long-distance rail travel proliferated. Writer Cy Warman created a wildly popular "True Tails of the Railroad" for McClure's magazine. Of course, wouldn't you know it, a cat was the subject of one of those articles. In that magazine piece, Wyman fondly recalls a railway worker who became inseparable from a stray black kitty. They often worked together, slept together, and traveled by train with one another, the black kit snoozing away on a bag of coal. The day came when the worker said goodbye to the railways to finally settle down, and the small cat awoke from her pile of coal when he called for her. One step from the train, however, and she decided to turn back. The kitty vagabond said her goodbyes to her cherished human companion and chose life a life of feline adventure on the railways instead. Sometimes, a cat's gotta do what a cat's gotta do...

Not everybody who rode the rails did so in first, second, or even third class. Around 1890, the term "hobo" was coined to refer to migrant workers or homeless vagrants who would hop on board and hide in freight carriages so they could ride across the country for free. Hoboes often sought places to stay between travels and would seek out homes where a cat lived. Such locations were supposedly marked with a special cat sign. This is because the presence of a cat often meant a kind-hearted woman who would be more likely to provide a warm cooked meal and place to sleep for those unfortunate hoboes. Whether in the 1800s or today, you should never underestimate the generosity of a cat lady.

Interestingly, one of the first American cats to travel by train was called Hobo, fittingly, as he was quite the traveler. He first rode the railway from San Francisco to New York City in 1868. I hope little Hobo packed a long enough ball of yarn to entertain himself for that long journey!

Life is a Highway

Nowadays, the average American drives about 150 miles a week and spends approximately an hour a day behind the wheel. People now take this for granted, but the American love affair with cars relied upon the cheap mass production of cars as pioneered by automotive pioneer Henry Ford and upon the development of a network of local and long-distance roads. Construction began on the first highways in the 1920s, eventually leading to the development of an interstate highway system under the Eisenhower Administration in the 1950s. While the car culture has given us unprecedented freedom of mobility (and drive-through fast-food joints—anyone taken their cat to one recently?), it has also led to increased pollution and, of course, traffic accidents, for both humans and for cats. Many cats are fatally injured each year, but one lucky cat named Rebel would survive the most frightening ride of his life.

In 2018, a van was spotted on Interstate 480 traveling 60 mph in Omaha, Nebraska, a gray and white fluffball clinging onto the roof for dear life. I imagine this to be quite difficult considering how sleek a car's rooftop is with nothing for claws to cling to. Passers-by captured the incident on video while trying to alert the driver of the little hitchhiker. Fortunately, the driver was able to pull over safely and retrieve the furry commuter from the roof. Thankfully, Rebel would be okay after this crazy ride, and I'm sure that this experience has taught his owner to check the roof of her car from now on before leaving her neighborhood. We sincerely hope that dear little Rebel has confined his adventures to the cat tower in his owner's living room since then.

Around 5.4 million cats are hit by cars each year, accounting for about 4% of their population. In percentages, that doesn't sound like much, but I know we all would like to see that number come down to zero! One way to reduce cat-cidents is to check your car before leaving any parking space, especially when living in an urban area with many street cats. Take special care to do so in winter, when animals might be sleeping beneath your car for warmth. Just give your hood a good smack-eroni to encourage any critters playing hide-and-seek to come on out!

Furthermore, be sure never to have any leaking antifreeze. This stuff is toxic to kitties! Check beneath your car for any wet spots on the ground that would indicate leakage. Finally, when driving at night, pay close attention as most cats tend to roam after dusk.

Places and Plants With Feline

Associations

Cat Claw Cactus—The Ultimate Low-Care Pet?

The Cat Claw Cactus is a succulent found in the Chihuahuan Desert of southeastern New Mexico and southwestern Texas. This chubby, round plant is covered in long, thin spikes that closely resemble a cat's claw, hence the name.

Growing in dry areas requiring little nutrients, these plants will even thrive within the crevices of rocks, making them pretty low-maintenance plants that don't require much attention. Some people say the same about cats as pets. They say that all felines need is food and water, to be left alone and that they're good to go. I don't know about you, but most cats of my acquaintance demand wet food and under-the-chin scratches every other hour, something that can get overwhelming at times. If you really do think cats are that hands-off, maybe try getting a cactus instead?

The Cat Park and Cat People of Salt Lake City

In Salt Lake City, Utah, there's a playground nestled within the Rose Park Neighborhood where locals of all ages, and species, come to play. Steenblik Park, also known as "The Cat Park," is home to four magnificent bronze cat statues positioned proudly to watch over the lush lawn. The attentive cat statues were created in honor of the many feline friends of the Steenblik family.

The Steenbliks immigrated to America from the Netherlands in 1903, establishing their dairy farm in the heart of Rose Park. It's no secret that cats like milk. Many found themselves right at home on the Steenblik dairy farm. The influential family would play a great role in the economy and growth of their city, supplying fresh dairy every morning to their happy Salt Lake City residents, including the ones with tails.

Sherrif Cat and The Catsburg Store

In the south of Durham County, North Carolina, you'll find a two-story farm in the style of a red barn. This structure dates from 1920 and features a giant black cat and the name "Catsburg" painted on its front canopy. While no longer open for business, the store remains as a landmark for the small, quaint town of Catsburg, named after their late Sheriff, "Cat" Belvin.

Sheriff Cat got his nickname thanks to his ability to sneak around unnoticed. This cat-like stealth helped him catch bootleggers and moonshiners during Prohibition. History doesn't record if he actually was a cat fan or what he thought of his feline nickname. However, some say that he himself was a purveyor of illegal hooch and that he hunted down his rivals while receiving a sheriff's salary. We're not sure the tale of shady double-dealing is true, but if it is, it sounds like a case of having your cream and eating it too…

American Pussy Willow

Willows make up the largest genus of tree-like plants in America. Cat lovers may be especially interested in a subspecies called the Pussy Willow that grows wild throughout the northern parts of the United States.

We're of the opinion that Mother Nature is a cat person. Such an opinion is borne out by the legend outlining the origin of the Pussy

Willow. It's said that a young litter of kittens once fell into the river while chasing butterflies. Ah, the poor darlings! Their mother cat desperately cried out for help, fearing that all was lost. Fortunately, a willow came to their aid sweeping one of its long branches into the water to bring the sad and soggy moggies back to shore. Now, every spring, the furry buds grow on the branches in the places where the kittens clung onto the willow for safety. And, in recognition of this valiant gesture, this compassionate tree has been dubbed a pussy willow. There might be other explanations for the name, but this is the one that we prefer, and we're sticking to this story.

Athletic Accomplishments

Basketball

During the 2017 NBA season, a lifelong enthusiast of the Philadelphia 76ers, Dennis Grove, sought a way to build morale during a dismal season that had many Sixers fans down in the dumps. Inspired by star guard Ben Simmons, who liked to carry his Savannah cats over his shoulders, Grove tweeted a picture of his hefty twelve-pound cat, Izzy, stating that he would raise his cat into the air if the Sixers won that night's game. Sure enough, they did win, and thus began the trend of #RaiseTheCat.

Philly sports fans continued the tradition of posing with their kitties raised to bring good luck to their favorite team. The trend became so successful that uber-fan Grove, who started the trend, even printed #RaiseTheCat onto t-shirts and generated $4,600 for the Philly PAWS No-Kill Animal Shelter and Morris Animal Refuge. The hashtag became the runner-up for the NBA's meme of the year.

Football

Just a few days after Halloween 2019, a black cat found his way onto the field at MetLife Stadium in the middle of a Monday Night Football game between the Dallas Cowboys and New York Giants. The kitty was first noticed by the Cowboys defensive end, Demarcus Lawrence. The athlete pointed out the feline running across the field, urging his fellow players to pause the game. This black cat's appearance turned out to be a good omen for the Cowboys, who trailed at 9-3 before his appearance. After the feline interruption, they went on to beat the Giants by a whopping 37-18. It looks like the witch who sent out this familiar must really be a Cowboys fan. The team went on to declare the kitty that night's Player of the Game with 117 Rushing Yards, two Touchdowns…and nine Lives.

Incredible Leaps to Safety

You've probably seen your cats make some pretty spectacular jumps, perhaps a four-foot leap onto the kitchen counter or a daring dive out of a tree, only to land with more grace than figure skater Kristi Yamaguchi. It could also be that your favorite furball is not quite so athletic. It's all right, they don't all have to win the Cat-o-lympics. We all know, however, that even our least athletic kitties have an innate ability to make some great jumps, and even falls, that surpass what any human can do.

In 1970s Florida, back when Senator Ken Myers held office, his own pet cat Andy fell from the sixteenth floor of his apartment, an astonishing fall of over 200 feet, and survived! The against-all-odds Andy went right into the Guinness Book of World Records for accomplishing the longest non-lethal feline fall. Those Florida cats sure are remarkable!

According to a 1987 study done by the Animal Medical Center of Manhattan, cats who fell from a distance higher than seven floors had more time to slow their speed and land more gently at the bottom of their leap. This is thanks to the parachuting that cats do with their bodies to gain air resistance. Pretty remarkable, I'd say! An important disclaimer from the hospital: The 132 cases of cats falling out of buildings were not purposely conducted by staff. Unfortunately, cats falling from high buildings is not uncommon in New York City, which has given researchers a solid sample to study.

Feline Folklore

Superstitions

You may have heard some common folk beliefs about cats: that they have nine lives or that a black cat crossing your path means bad luck. There are indeed many superstitions that date back as far as colonial America. Early European settlers even looked to their felines for weather forecasts. It was said that a cat with his back toward the fireplace meant a cold snap to come. Not only could these prescient felines *fur*-see the weather but your fortune as well. If a cat washed her face in front of several people, the first person with whom the cat made eye contact, would soon be married. Forget about throwing your single friends a bouquet at your wedding; just invite them round the next time your cat starts washing its face. For those of you who have front porches, be aware that a cat grooming himself on the front porch supposedly meant that a clergyman would come a-calling. Is there no end to our cats' powers? They can find single women husbands and summon up clergymen. Quite remarkable, wouldn't you agree?

You should know that black cats aren't the only unlucky ones. While seeing a white cat during the day, or in your dreams, is a sign of good luck, seeing them at night means bad luck. And any cat, regardless of color, sitting on a grave supposedly means that the deceased is possessed by the devil. Two cats fighting near the grave, or an ill person's bedside, indicates a battle between an angel and a devil for their soul. In the American South, those who drown a cat will be punished by the devil, and quite rightly so!

Due to lingering superstitions related to them, even today, black cats often face the most discrimination and harm. However, black cats also have a gene that happens to give them a better immune system, making them the healthiest of cats. So, who's the lucky one?

Among the Pennsylvania German community, placing a cat into a baby's cradle was supposed to help grant your wishes. We don't know whether babies were comfortable with the furry, luck-bestowing interlopers in their cribs. The Pennsylvania Germans also believed that feeding a cat from your shoe would help with pre-wedding jitters! I wonder how many anxious brides actually tried this one on for size!

Folklore indicates that any kitten born in the month of May will be a witch's cat. Considering most cats are born during the spring, the likelihood of this occurring is quite high. Another folk tradition has it that if a witch moves into a house, black cats will refuse to reside there. So, if your black kitty spends a lot of time outdoors, it might be time to take your broomstick for a test drive!

The Cactus Cat

When the frontiersmen of the American West journeyed through the deserts, they created the tale of the Cactus Cat. The Cactus Cat had sharp, thorny hair that was especially long and spiky at the ears. His tail was bent and branched, just like a cactus, and on his front legs, blades of bone protruded to slash at giant cacti for the cool sap within. The cactus sap was quick to ferment, filling the cat's belly with intoxicating mush. High as a kite, the drunken Cactus Cat darted around the desert, uttering the most horrendous of screams. Gosh, darn it, that sounds exactly like my neighbor's cat!

A Capitol Affair

The U.S. Capitol Building is supposed to be home to quite a few supernatural apparitions. The ghost of John Quincy Adams and of some Civil War soldiers have been spotted roaming the halls at night, mumbling incoherently to themselves…as opposed to many of our politicians who do so during the day! There are stories of a Demon Cat, also known as "D.C."… Get it? During the post-Civil War era, the night watchmen reported seeing a black cat, which isn't that unusual. However, this remarkable cat grew to the size of a panther and pounced on one of the guards! The poor man fought to get the cat off him, and as he was doing so, the phantom feline suddenly vanished into thin air, just as quickly as he had appeared…

It's said that the ghostly kitty reappears at times of national tragedy, as well as presidential changeovers. It seems the fiendish D.C. feline wouldn't miss the pomp and ceremony of an inauguration for the world! Tiny pawprints in the concrete that are so subtle as to be almost invisible have been claimed to be D.C.'s way of making his presence known.

Some Notable Cats (and Some Pretty Cool Humans)

How much do you love your dear kitties? Whether it's one extra belly rub or putting out warm blankets for our furry neighbors in the streets, I'm sure we all do our part to make this world a little more comfy for kitties.

One person who went far above and beyond in the service of cats was Cleveland Armory. This upstanding man devoted his life to the advocacy of animal rights. Best known as the co-founder of the Humane Society in 1962, he also established the Black Beauty Ranch to shelter abused animals. If that weren't enough, he also created the Fund for Animals that rescued animals scheduled for extermination by the US Department of Defense and the National Park Service. In 1987, he published a number of bestselling novels about his adopted cat, Polar Bear, which charmed the nation. Mr. Armory, we and our kitties salute you and all your magnificent deeds!

Up until relatively recently, many blind kitties were routinely euthanized because it was believed that they couldn't function well enough to be adopted out. Unfortunately, this mistaken belief still persists at many shelters, which is why the Blind Cat Rescue & Sanctuary was created. The rescue was founded in 2005 in St Pauls, North Carolina, by a mother and daughter team volunteering at their local shelter, which was where they encountered their first blind cat in need of care. A man came in with a black and white cat who was only six weeks old. He couldn't care for the kitty, and the shelter refused to take him in either! That's when the two stepped up to take him in and name him Louie.

Louie turned out to be a loveable and snuggly big boy with all the crazy antics and powerful purrs of any seeing cat! Nothing stopped him from climbing trees and getting on top of cabinets except, well, laziness and a few added pounds.

It didn't take long for the kindly mother and daughter to take in a second, third-, and fourth-blind kitty as they started to realize just how many were in need. It made sense for them to eventually create their own charity that homes not just blind kitties but also those with missing legs or who test positive for FIV or leukemia. The Blind Cat Rescue & Sanctuary now houses about one hundred cats, which can be sponsored at any time or watched online through their website's video portals! Check out these cuties. You'll want to see how they frolic on their giant hamster wheels! It's truly a sight to behold.

All the way back in 1929, a San Diego, California organization called the Animal Rescue League was established by a group of locals who used their own money to adopt every animal from the city's shelters that used euthanasia. Following the stock market crash, the rescue's funds would become depleted, but a woman named Maude Erwin would care for twenty cats on her own and, with the help of friends, raise funding to rebuild the shelter.

With the goal of ensuring every abandoned or unwanted animal would have a home, the organization would grow to become a no-kill shelter called Friends of Cats. The shelter houses over three hundred cats on average, with separate cottages for feral cats, those fearful of humans, or those living with feline leukemia. They take in kittens and cats of all ages who are either adopted or stay there for life.

As well as living well, some outstanding kitties live extraordinarily long lives. The oldest cat to ever live was a white tabby mix from San Antonio, Texas, named Creme Puff. Texas is, after all, the home of the biggest, the bravest, and—the longest-lived—we guess. She lived to be thirty-eight years and three days old, which is approximately 110 in human years. Her owner, Jake Perry, says that it was thanks to a diet of dry food mixed with broccoli, eggs, turkey bacon, and coffee *with* cream, of course. He also gave her an eye dropper with red wine every two days to help her with healthy blood circulation. Keep in mind though, while some studies have indicated that red wine may improve heart health in humans, veterinarians emphasize that alcohol should **not** be given to cats due to numerous health hazards it may pose. Who knows, Crème Puff might have lived even longer had she been a teetotaler…

Jake Perry was also the owner of another Guinness World Record holder, Grandpa Rex Allen, a Sphynx Devon-Rex who lived to be thirty-four years and two months old. If you're wondering what Perry's secret was to rearing cats who lived so long, there might be some useful pointers to glean from his cats' daily routine. The cats liked to roam around outside in Perry's enclosed backyard, and when they were inside, they liked to watch plenty of nature documentaries in his home theater. You might want to start changing the channel for your own kitties. Even if it didn't increase their lifespan, I'm sure they'd appreciate some of that fascinating wildlife programming. I know I personally can't get enough of David Attenborough.

Boo, Hiss! Those Cat Haters

It's not easy being beautiful, popular, and adored by millions. With the cat lovers also come the haters…

Isadora Duncan

Isadora Duncan (1877-1927) is better known as a world-famous American dancer. However, her character is besmirched by a strong streak of animal cruelty. This extra evil step-sister of *Cruella de Vil* lived next door to a cat sanctuary. Some kitties would cross into her backyard, and Duncan felt it appropriate to order her servants to kill the cats!

It might take a while, but karma has a way of punishing us for our past evils. So, beware all those who anger the cat gods… Duncan was thrown from a fast-moving car in 1927. Her scarf caught beneath the wheel, strangling her at the neck. It is not recorded whether any kitties witnessed her unfortunate demise...

Rockwell Sayre

In 1921, headlines in the newspaper read "Shall We Kill Every Cat in the U.S.?" Millionaire investment broker from Chicago, Rockwell Sayre, also known as "the world's most assiduous cat hater," began a movement to exterminate all cats

The crazy banker compared cats to cockroaches and mosquitoes, even claiming that they would "jump upon a corpse and tear the face of the dead!" Paw-don me, but I would like to see a fact-check for that claim. Eventually, Sayre would die before the end of his campaign. Apparently, he was shot by his own son. Mmm, sounds like a nice, normal family… Despite additional funds set aside in Sayre's will to continue his quest for extermination, the cat-killing fever finally ended.

It Ain't What You Say, It's The Way That Ya Say It!

Gotta Love That Slang

Just as they're ever-present in our homes, America's felines are an integral part of our language, as the following explanations of common phrases will confirm.

The phrase "cool cats" was originally a musical term. Jazz music started as being "hot," highly energetic, and rhythmic. The calmer, more relaxed style that later evolved was then referred to as "cool." And "cats" were used to refer to jazz players and lovers since they often enjoyed the music late at night when only cats were awake. Some of us can attest to that. My cat is always up running around at midnight. I'll bet my downstairs neighbor thinks he must be doing the lindy hop. What can I say? I've got a hip jazz cat!

"Scaredy cat," or earlier known as "fraidy cat," popped up in newspapers as early as 1897 with a poem published in a newspaper called The Chronicle that included the line "Tear his trousers, spoil his hat—Fraidy cat!"

"The cat's meow" was originally used by the fabulous flappers of the 1920s to describe anything fashionable or extravagant. These ladies were all about risqué and eye-catching finery—that just *meows* cat, doesn't it?

Cats are still incredibly relevant in today's pop culture. Hip hop artists, such as Kanye West, have even made "meow meow," a trending slang term referring to club drug ecstasy because the drug's official name is "methylmethcathinone," aka MM-CAT. With the amount of "meow meow meows" I'm sure you hear late at night, you might conclude that your cat was on such a mind-altering substance, one apart from dear old catnip that is.

American Proverbs

"You will always be lucky if you know how to make friends with strange cats." This proverb dates to colonial times. It was believed that captivating, endearing personalities would attract others (including cats) and thereby find themselves prosperous because of how their popularity attracted others to do business with them. I better tell my friend whose house is always besieged by stray cats that millions of dollars are headed his way!

In 1854, American humorist and writer Seba Smith first penned the proverb, "There is more than one way to skin a cat." In case you shudder any time you hear this phrase, don't worry; she's referring to a catfish whose epidermis it is possible to remove in various ways before cooking it. Phew! I'm sure glad no felines were harmed in the making of that phrase...

From the 1930s through the 1960s, Red Barber was the guy to listen to in sports broadcasting. He gave the hottest play-by-plays for the Major League Baseball teams. During those four decades, he coined the saying, "in the catbird seat," to refer to someone having the greater advantage or upper hand of the game. So, let's hope we all end up in the catbird seat...

The Name Game

Did you know that the letter "M" is the most common letter used in cat names? Mmmmm, I can't quite figure out why. Could it be all that ME-owing on our furry friends' part? Cut that out, Mittens, Minnie--

and you too, Midnight!

As of 2021, the two most popular cat names for girls are Luna and Bella. For boys, it's Oliver or Leo. As to the popularity of the name Luna, there are maybe a few factors at play. Luna means "moon" in Spanish. In ancient symbolism, Egyptians related cats to the moon goddess, Bastet. Owners and veterinarians have also claimed that cats display exaggerated behaviors of restlessness, mischief, or even hiding during a full moon. One long-term study in 2007 found that cat visits to the vet increased by 23% over the course of a full moon. Bella means pretty, and the reason for its popularity should be obvious. Who wouldn't be smitten with the lovely looks of their darling new kitten?

As for Oliver, the popularity of this name might be due to the little orange stray of the same name from the 1988 Disney film *Oliver and Company*, an animated adaptation of the Charles Dickens story *Oliver Twist*. How could anyone not fall for that name after watching a tiny, orphaned kitty named Oliver learn the ways of the streets with his homeless canine friends? As for the popularity of Leo, we'd imagine pet parents are thinking of how their fierce little mites resemble the mighty wild lion, none other than *Panthera leo*.

Strange and Spooky

In 1930 the nation was fascinated to learn the tale of a psychic Persian kitty named Napoleon, also known as the Weather Prophet of Baltimore, Maryland. This fluffy white clairvoyant belonged to Mrs. Fanny de Shields, who often witnessed his powers at work. Before it rained, Napoleon would lie flat on his stomach, his front paws extended straight in front of him, while he pressed his face flat against the floor. That must have been quite the sight to behold!

Anyhow, during a month-long drought, the official weather forecast had predicted continuing dry weather…but the furry prophet declared otherwise. As soon as he assumed his "rainmaker" pose, Mrs. De Shields contacted the *Baltimore Sun* newspaper to advise them to change the forecasts. They ignored her but were later to regret not paying attention. When Napoleon's premonition was proven to be true, all of Baltimore finally recognized the psychic's true powers. And for the next six years until his passing, the Weather Prophet's forecasts continued to be published in the newspapers.

Another keen kitty who predicted the weather was a mother who had just given birth to a full litter inside a barn in Lawrence, Kansas. One morning, the farmer noticed that one of the recently-born kittens was missing. Come the next day, another one was gone. Then, all the kittens and their mother were missing from the barn. The farmer feared there must have been a predator lurking nearby who had taken the poor little kitties. But that wasn't the case. Soon enough, a massive tornado pummeled the town, completely destroying the barn. The following morning, the farmer heard from his neighbor several miles away that the mother cat had relocated herself and her babies to his barn, which was completely unaffected by the disaster…

When nuclear physicist, Dr. Ruehl, was a graduate student at UCLA in California, he had a cat named Simba, who always rushed toward the phone just seconds before it rang. Dr. Ruehl conducted many experiments to find how this could be possible. Was there a frequency emitted at the start of a ring that only cats could hear? And why was Simba only able to use his powers if his owner was also present in the room? Try as hard as he could, Dr. Ruehl never could find any scientific reason for this feline psychic phenomenon.

Sonya Fitzpatrick, TV host of Animal Planet's Pet Psychic, has stated on her program that cats conceive of their feelings as pictures, which images they can telepathically send to each other, and apparently, to humans as well. If you're *feline* curious to learn more about these paranormal powers and practice them with your kitty, check out Fitzpatrick's book *Communicating with Your Cat* as well as Missy Dizick's *Test Your Cat's Psychic Powers*. Make sure to harness your kitty's psychic powers for good, won't you? You know, like predicting the lottery and other benevolent endeavors. They do say charity begins at home, after all!

E Purr-i-bus Unum: Some Fascinating Stories of Popular Cat Breeds

What Is a Breed Anyhow?

What constitutes a cat breed is open to interpretation. Encyclopedia Britannica recognizes only seventeen different breeds, whereas the largest genetic registry of pedigreed cats in the world, the International Cat Association, recognizes seventy-one! The largest American Association recognizes only forty-four… I guess this all goes to prove that there are really no hard and fast rules when it comes to cats. Yep, try getting cats to follow *any* guidelines…

Still, maybe some of these breeds might be *fur-miliar* to you! A few of the most popular kinds of cats in America today are Maine Coons, Persians, Ragdolls, and American Curls. Of course, many of the cats we see today are a happy mix of many different official breeds, and that just makes them even more unique, and not a hair less lovable!

These various breeds of America's fabulous kitties are adored not just in our homes but also in glamorous cat shows across the world. Here they bask in the attention elsewhere bestowed on their human equivalents, the supermodels who strut their very own catwalks. The first major cat show in America was held in 1895 at Madison Square Garden in New York City, where cats were judged according to a range of breed standards, not just the judges' personal preferences. The champion that year was a Maine Coon. Soon after, more litters of cat clubs would pop up, spreading out to Chicago. By 1900, the first studbook and registry would finally be published, and in 1910, the NCC officers would meet with sixteen other cat clubs to establish the Governing Council of the Cat Fancy, regulating all shows in America and maintaining one single registry.

With the Great Depression and World War II, the shows experienced a dip, but just as cats have nine lives, so do the shows! In 1954, cat fancies would be revived, with more and more associations being born. Since then, they've gone from strength to strength. Read on for some fascinating tidbits about the breeds who grace these popular shows.

American Shorthairs, Top of the Heap?

Believed to be a mix of the European Shorthair and the Egyptian Cat, they most likely arrived in America with the pilgrims in 1620. A diary account from American shorthair breeder Kay McQuillen's great-great-grandmother, Mrs. Heaney, tells of her own feline laying a fresh litter of shorthairs on Plymouth Rock as soon as the Mayflower landed. These cats were originally a part of the crew's pest control, and as more and more of them sailed to the New World, they began to populate and spread across the country.

Domestic Shorthairs, The Also Ran's?

The story of the Domestic Shorthair is that they are a mix of different ancestries and have at times been dismissed as mere mutts. These cats are descendants of the American Shorthairs who mated with other breeds that found their way to America.

Near the end of the nineteenth century, these felines started appearing at cat shows, but it was hard for them to compete with some of the more glamorous foreign breeds. You know how those pageant politics go. Rumors circulated that this breed came (gasp, shudder!) mainly from animal shelters. This class found themselves not being benched at some cat shows, cages not available for them, and not even trophies or ribbons provided for them! How snobbish this was, and frankly totally against that egalitarian American spirit of everyone getting a shot at the American Dream!

By the beginning of the twentieth century, the Domestic Shorthair would finally be registered as a pedigree cat thanks to Shorthair breeder Jane Cathcart and her showstoppers Champion Belle and Buster Brown. In the 1960s, these Shorthair enthusiasts would then decide to change the name of the breed from Domestic Shorthair to American Shorthair as a strategy to establish their breed as one deserving of a more illustrious pedigree.

Nowadays, the term Domestic Shorthair is used for mixed shelter cats who resemble their fancier feline first-cousins. Meanwhile, those who can prove their genetic pedigree are officially registered as American Shorthairs.

Maine Coons, A Somewhat Fuzzy History

Some highly fanciful accounts have it that the Maine Coon is descended from some high-falutin' French fluffsters. These posh progenitors were supposedly shipped from France to America in preparation for Marie Antoinette's hoped-for escape in the wake of the French Revolution. If you were fleeing to another country, your cats would also be first on your list to save, too.

Others believe that Maine Coons are the result of shorthairs breeding with longhairs that came from the Vikings. There's also the belief that a raccoon mated with a cat to create the Maine Coon. Well, of all the "tall tails" I've ever heard, that one beats the bunch!

However they came about, this breed might be the oldest one referred to in written accounts. It seems that the thick coat that they are known for is a quite a helpful characteristic for living through cold winters. Their distinctive fur is heavy, water-resistant, and glossy. It grows longer around the stomach, presumably as protection from the snow, and shorter on top, perhaps so as not to be caught in the underbrush.

Maine Coons are muscular cats with heavy-set males weighing up to twenty pounds, and females eight to twelve pounds. In the late 1800s, these cats competed at the New York Cat Show and became winning showstoppers. While their pride of position among longhairs was eclipsed by Persians for some time, the Maine Coon's popularity would be revived in the 1950s, and they would even become the official state cat of Maine in 1985, an honor long overdue, perhaps?

Those Laidback Ragdolls

In California during the far-out 1960s, a free-roaming longhair fell in love with a beautiful Birman, and together, they gave birth to a kitty who was named Daddy War Bucks. This groovy cat would go on to be the father of the Ragdoll breed.

The Ragdoll cat gets its name from its tendency to go limp in a person's arms when held, exactly like a child's treasured ragdoll would. This breed is known for being large—the heftiest of all domestic breeds— affectionate and easy-going. Baker, the breeder responsible for creating the Ragdoll, specifically chose to breed Daddy War Bucks for his unusually calm temperament. With a gentle and tame nature, these cats come to have strong, loving attachments to their owners.

Peace and love to all, man...

California Spangleds, The Controversial Glamorpusses

The California Spangled Domestic cat breed was introduced to the public on the glossy cover of a 1986 Neiman Marcus Christmas catalog. With a remarkable appearance akin to a miniature leopard, this new arrival attracted much attention—and indeed much controversy. It was Hollywood screenwriter, Paul Casey, who created this dramatic new arrival to the world of American cats. On a work assignment in the Olduvai Gorge Museum in Africa, Casey was horrified to discover the widespread poaching of endangered leopards in the area.

Upon returning to California, Casey was unable to forget the gorgeous spotted felines he got to gaze on in the wild, so he set out to create an elaborate breeding program that would produce a domestic breed that embodied the beauty of the leopard, one that might discourage the public from wanting to wear coats made from such glorious creatures. However, his ode to the leopard was viewed as distasteful and dubious, as he introduced it to the world as a purr-chasable option via a department store catalog where they would be sold alongside luxury clothing and other high-end accoutrements. To make matters worse, the cat was priced at $1,400, to be sold "in any color clients may desire to match their clothes or *home decor*" as an exclusive "His/Her Christmas Package."

The Humane Society immediately called for a boycott of the department store, Neiman Marcus, even starting picket protests, stating that living creatures shouldn't be "made to order" as a high-priced toy or accessory. The breed's enthusiasts held fast, defending the spangleds as raising awareness of their leopard cousins' endangered status.

The politics of a dramatic origin story aside, this breed's origins are a story of iconoclasm, glamour, and financial high stakes that equals any great American novel. "The Great Cat-sby" anyone?

The Russians Who Came West

Featuring consistently on America's most popular cat breeds lists, this stunning blue cat with bright green eyes was originally only seen in Russia until their first cat show appearance at The Crystal Palace in England in 1875. It was after this show that the cat would move westwards in any numbers. However, by the end of World War II, the Russian Blue would become a rare species to the point that crossbreeding began with Siamese cats, which would explain why some pointed blue cats can be found! Soon after, Americans would mix Scandinavian and British Russian Blues to create the modern Russian Blue. Not so surprising… Running low on imports? America will produce its own!

They are very gentle and shy kitties who are sensitive to their owner's emotions. It's rumored that the breed is descended from the cats who had belonged to the Russian Czars since the sixteenth century! That would explain such a classy purr-sona. Well, up until you play a game of fetch with them. You see, they're almost dog-like in their ability to retrieve, something other breeds might consider—tsk, tsk—quite "un-cat-like!"

Siamese If You Please

The story of how Siamese cats came to the US is a rather interesting one. In 1878, David Sickles, who was stationed as a diplomat in Bangkok, got word that the First Lady of the United States Mrs. Hayes was a cat lover. Siam is the ancient name of Thailand, and Sickles had noticed rather striking cats in Bangkok who were known as Siamese. He took it upon himself to send one of these alluring-looking cats as a gift to the 19th president's wife. This seems to be the first documented instance of a cat of this breed reaching American shores. We have correspondence between Sickles and Mrs. Hayes as our evidence. It took two months for "Siam" (for that was the cat's name) to arrive in Washington. The president's 12-year-old daughter Fanny was particularly excited about having a new kitty in her home. Unfortunately, nine months after coming to America, Siam became rather ill. The president's family was out of town when this happened. The White House staff desperately tried to build up Siam's strength by offering an array of treats ranging from fish to duck to cream and even some oysters. Nothing worked, so the president's personal doctor was sent for. The kind, pet-loving Dr. Baxter advised beef tea and milk at intervals of three hours. Sadly, even though the good doctor took the cat to his home for direct supervision, the unfortunate Siam died. Nowadays, Siamese cats consistently feature on the list of most popular cat breeds in the US and have become part of our lives as well as our popular culture. Who can forget the singing Siamese cats from that animated Disney classic, "Lady and the Tramp?" In that funny ditty, the Siamese songsters come across as rather haughty. It's no wonder they have this reputation because Thai folklore tells us that when a member of the Thai royal family died, the spirit would pass to their pet Siamese cat, and the cat would then spend the rest of its days being pampered in a temple with monks hovering to fulfill its every wish. Present-day American owners report that these kitties crave attention and are very vocal about getting their needs met. Well, if you're cat royalty, you should get every whim catered to!

American Curl

It was the summer of 1981 when a female cat with long black hair showed up on the California doorstep of Joe and Grace Ruga, looking for a bite to eat and a place to stay. She had distinctive ears, with a slight curl forward at the tips. It didn't take long for her to become a member of the family and sport the name Shulamith. Since the Rugas weren't very familiar with cat breeds, they had no idea exactly how unique Shulamith was.

Shulamith would eventually find a tomcat that she liked, and together they had their own offspring who ended up being born with pe-curl-iar ears like their mom! More and more litters would be gifted to friends and family. One of the recipients was familiar with pedigree cats and had read how the ears of Scottish Folds were what set them apart as a breed in their own right. At that point, the odd genetic mutation would finally be documented and recognized as an official brand-new American breed!

Requiring only one copy of the gene to recreate the curly eared trait, the breed was simple to reproduce healthily. They are commonly referred to as the Peter Pan of felines because they often retain the same personalities as they had as kittens.

Gathering Places—for Humans and Cats Alike!

Sammy's Bowery Follies, New York, 1947.

Hanging Out in Bars and Taverns

Founded in 1854, McSorley's Old Ale House on Seventh Street in New York City was not simply a place for humans to sup and find sustenance; it offered a refuge for street cats as well. The tavern's owner, Bill McSorley, was a gruff man that no one wanted to mess with, but he had the warmest heart for these furry felines, caring for as many as eighteen at one time. In 1919, Bill told newspapers that he was keeping alive a tradition of kindness to cats started by his father, the bar's founder, who told him that it cost less to keep a cat than to pay a plumber since cats kept mice from gnawing through the bar's infrastructure.

Fast forward to Manhattan during the Prohibition, former bartender Jack Bleek was running a Manhattan Speakeasy called the Opera Cafe on Seventh Avenue. Just as he was about to put up a *Help Wanted* sign for a good mouser, he noticed an orphaned little black and white kitty out in the street. Bleek took her in, cleaned her up, and gave her a filling dinner before presumably tucking her into a comfortable bed for the night. The very next day, the grateful kitty thanked him with a mouse at his feet.

It didn't take long for this formerly frail feline to truly show her mettle. She set about chasing rats before they had a chance to nibble on patrons' shoes. Yep, those rapacious "Noo Yawk" rodents were that aggressive! She would watch them for up to four hours at a time until they came out, thinking it was safe and that the pesky cat would have given up and moved on. But they were wrong—so, so wrong. Minnie always finished the job. She had the place clean of rodents within six months. When Minnie passed away in 1934, Bleek told the *New York Herald Tribune* reporter all about the hard work she did to keep the joint safe for illegal boozing. "It was a tough job," he said, wiping his tears away. "The rats used to gang her, but her paws moved like lightning, and she could punch like Dempsey!" (referring to the much-admired heavyweight boxer of that era).

Finding Fine Feline Lodgings

New York's Algonquin Hotel was *the* place to drink and to lodge for the most notable literary and Broadway talents, including literary wit Dorothy Parker, known for her exceptionally catty quips. But did you know about its fabulous feline residents? In 1927, a fuzzy little stray, who was certainly lost, took a step in the right direction when he passed through the entrance of the luxurious hotel. Founder and owner of the hotel, Frank Case, could not resist adopting him and naming him Billy. Billy enjoyed a full life as a pampered puss in the hotel to his very last days. And when he went, all the patrons of the hotels mourned his loss.

Call it luck, or a star who knew it was his time to shine, but just two days after Billy had gone, another homeless cat appeared at the Algonquin. We all know how quickly word gets around of a vacancy on Broadway. New Yorkers are always on the lookout for a chance to get on in the world. While most would have considered the ragamuffin an unwanted intruder, Case felt the grief in his heart begin to heal as soon as he picked up the fluffy orange tabby. He knew there was something special about this kitty.

It didn't take long for Rusty to learn the ropes of his new life as a distinguished feline gentleman. Every morning, he ran straight to Mrs.

Case for a proper grooming as soon as he saw her take out the hairbrush. Then he would go out to the elevator. If it was going up, he did not go in. This is because he would wait until it was going down to the lobby. Here, at street level, Rusty was in the midst of all the check-ins and check-outs. Relishing his new life of luxury, he slept wherever he wanted, whether it was the reception desk or the middle of the floor. He also made sure to demand his shot of milk at the bar every evening. After all, who could begrudge him a sundowner after a demanding day in the center of the hustle and bustle? As befitted someone who was always on stage, he would soon be granted a new moniker to better fit his important status, that of Hamlet.

Almost a century later, the hotel has maintained the tradition of homing a feline star-in-residence. There have been twelve, and counting, so far. Every gentleman is named Hamlet, and every lady, Matilda. We're sure a host of hopeful kitties from Manhattan's streets daydream of their chance to walk through the fabulous doors of the Algonquin hotel and take their rightful place in such gracious and historic surroundings. In the cutthroat world of Manhattan real estate, you have to claw at every chance you can get!

Now, That's Entertainment!

Street Purr-formers & Circus Cats

Those who perform outside to an assembled crowd have a long history, dating back to medieval minstrels and the troupes of traveling players who were common in Shakespeare's day. One talented man and his nimble felines who are contributing to this legendary legacy are often to be found at the Hilton Pier in Key West, Florida, where they regularly dazzle locals and tourists alike. We're speaking of talented cat acrobats Oscar, Cossette, Chopin, George, Sara, and Mandarine…and their human ringmaster, Dominique "The Catman" LeFort. Whether they are jumping through flaming hoops, running across the balance beam, or otherwise being acrobatically inclined, these cats are out to impress. The French-accented ringmaster's lion-tamer garments and shaggy blonde mane lend the whole scene the dramatic razzmatazz of Las Vegas.

Still, there are other "cat entertainers" who haven't provided their audiences with quite as much honest-to-goodness excitement as do Le Fort and his felines. I'm referring to none other than the infamous American impresario P.T. Barnum. The Barnum & Bailey Circus founder was a renowned showman and celebrated hoaxer of the late 1800s. The saying, "There's a sucker born every minute" is widely attributed to him, although others say it was used about the showman rather than uttered by him. Whatever the case, Barnum certainly had some nerve when it came to promoting his attractions. He once advertised that he was displaying a "genuine" cherry-colored cat, leading to a line of curious patrons enthusiastically purchasing tickets to gaze upon such an unusually hued feline. His audience ended up sorely disappointed when they found themselves staring at a rather unremarkable, everyday coal black cat. When they irately demanded refunds, Barnum turned a deaf ear to their pleas, pointing out matter-of-factly that some cherries are indeed black!

Kitties in The Comic Strips

An American pastime enjoyed almost universally by both children and adults in pre-digital days was reading the newspaper comic strips. Sipping a coffee at the breakfast table, parents could enjoy a wholesome laugh with their families, all in just a few short minutes. Before radio or TV, it was the ultimate form of accessible light entertainment. The first nationally popular comic strip was *The Yellow Kid*, which made its appearance in American newspapers in the 1890s. It was soon joined by others until these illustrated stories released in installments grew to become what were known affectionately as "the funny pages," with newspapers vying to outdo each other in the size and drawing power of the strips they had syndicated. These sections gave a light-hearted and welcome diversion to the regular news. It wouldn't take long for the family cat to want in on the fun, too.

Krazy Kat first appeared in 1910 in cartoonist George Herriman's newspaper strip, *The Dingbat Family*. Krazy Kat would later play a careless tom in his own 1913 series, starring himself and Ignatz, the short-tempered mouse. Their relationship would be a strange one as Ignatz would often throw bricks at Krazy Kat's head when he walked by, which Krazy Kat strangely thought to be simply the mouse's way of showing affection…While Krazy Kat couldn't seem to win the heart of Ignatz, he surely did win over those of literary heavyweights E. E.

Cummings and James Joyce, who were huge fans of the character.

Krazy Kat's modern feline cartoon equivalent is probably to be found wherever lasagna is served. Garfield, the chubby carb-munching cat, first appeared in newspapers in 1978, and despite his laziness and cynical demeanor, he would come to be loved by not just Americans but by people all over the world. Printed in a dozen languages and distributed by over 2,500 papers, *Garfield* holds the Guinness World Record as the most syndicated comic strip. Although easily reduced to an array of goofy stereotypes, Garfield's deeper side has left us with some insightful sayings to ponder. Consider this pearl of wisdom: "They say a cat always lands on his feet, but they don't say how painful it is." This may be true of cats everywhere, but I'm sure that at the end of the day, it can relate to any one of us as well. Garfield, you old curmudgeonly rascal, you have certainly won our hearts, but you have intrigued our intellects as well.

Cats and The Early Days of Radio

At the dawn of the radio era, people picked up radio signals by touching a long thin wire against a crystal to create a connection for radio signals. This long wire was called "the cat's whisker." This was a giant step in the story of human progress, yet another leap forward that has a fascinating feline association.

The popularity of radio grew rapidly in America during the 1920s, and by the mid-1930s, radios had become a staple in over 60% of the nation's homes. For the first time, people could have live, "streaming" entertainment and news in their homes, even if it was only of the audio variety. It wouldn't take long for our attention-seeking friends to get their paws on it, too! In 1944 Smilin' Ed McConnell started hosting a kid's radio show called *The Buster Brown Gang* featuring none other than a violin-playing kitty named Midnight, who only knew how to say one word: Niiiiiice!

Children across the nation tried to imagine how a musical, speaking cat could even be *pawsible*. However, they finally did get to feast their eyes on the black cat in action when the show made it to television a decade later. Midnight would play classic songs like "Three Blind Mice" and "Jesus Loves Me" with his furry paws on a piano and a little drumming hamster named Squeaky to back him up. It sounds like first-class All-American entertainment to me!

Hooray for Hollywood!

With their naturally proud cat-titude and undeniable star purr-esence, it was inevitable that felines would play major roles in Tinseltown's triumphs. In fact, long before Hollywood was even established, cats made a screen splash in 1894 with none other than Thomas Edison producing a film short entitled "The Boxing Cats," complete with cats in a dinky little boxing ring swatting it out like miniature Rocky's. Probably the first appearance in a longer film format would be by a stray kitty named Pepper who made his way as a very young kitten, from his momma cat's nest up through the floorboards of the Keystone Studios soundstage during a 1912 shooting. This cat was literally born to be in showbusiness! The director, Mack Sennett, would roll with it and to paraphrase that Hollywood one-liner, "the kit stayed in the picture!" Not only did Pepper make her way on screen as an impish kitten, but she also went on to have quite a career in the silent movies, acting in over a dozen pictures, alongside silent film greats Charlie Chaplin and Fatty Arbuckle. Talk about clawing your way to the top! However, unlike her human counterparts, she didn't really reap the material awards, only earning $35 a role, not a whole lot of kitty kibble, even back in the day…

Another great kitty from the early days of film was Felix the Cat. This fine fellow was none other than the first animated film star of any species… Modeled after Charlie Chaplin, this comical cat starred in 150 silent cartoons, inspired numerous products festooned with his likeness, and in 1930 was the first still image broadcast on commercial US television. The TV age started with a cat! Who knew? At his peak, Felix was as popular as Mickey Mouse. What's more, he continues to be relevant right now. Every year since 1927, Felix has had a massive balloon in the Macy's Thanksgiving Day Parade, broadcast live into homes across America, quite an incredible feat of longevity for a star who had his debut back in the era of silent films. Later on, Felix was joined by *Tom and Jerry*, the ever-bickering cat and mouse duo, as well as Sylvester from *The Looney Tunes* series. Lest anyone might dare think these cartoon felines were just run-of-the-mill, your cat might remind you that the 1947 short *Tweetie Pie* won an Oscar, and *Tom and Jerry* won seven of those ultimate film accolades!

And The Award Goes To…

Although Hollywood is all about the box office, even the most self-confident of performers craves recognition from their peers. Hence, the plethora of award shows in showbusiness. The American Humane Society even created the PATSY Award, the Picture Animal Top Star

Award, after a horse was sadly killed while filming a Western. Finally, the hard work, talent, (and sacrifices) of animal actors would rightly be recognized. This furry equivalent of the Oscars had its first ceremony hosted by President Ronald Reagan at the Carthay Circle Theater. So, *drumroll please*…ladies and gentlemen, let's take a look at perhaps the greatest of America's *fur*-avorite feline award winners… We're speaking of none other than the inimitable Orangey who starred in a now largely forgotten cat classic, that of Rhubarb.

The film tells the story of a stray named Rhubarb, who is adopted by the eccentric millionaire owner of the Brooklyn Loons baseball team. Gotta love those All-American rags-to-riches stories… When the millionaire promptly passes away, Rhubarb inherits his entire estate and the sports team. However, he then becomes the target of a kitty-napping. For shame! Some people are just so jealous of cats and their lucky breaks. The kitty was eventually rescued, but not before lots of kooky shenanigans. Orangey would become the only animal to ever win *two* PATSYs, one as Rhubarb and one for his iconic 1962 role alongside Audrey Hepburn in *Breakfast at Tiffany's*. As befits a great star, Orangey was rumored to have major creative differences with other actors, often biting and scratching them. Sometimes he would flee the set, so guard dogs were posted at the entrance to make sure he didn't disappear completely. It's said that his final screen appearance was in 1967 when he played an uncredited role alongside Eartha Kitt, who was starring as Catwoman in the TV series Batman. What a role to choose for your departure from show business, staring alongside the inimitable Eartha! Orangey's career was so remarkable that he is the subject of a 2020 short documentary titled "The Hardest Working Cat in Showbusiness."

The PATSY awards would end in 1986 due to a lack of funding. Maybe it's time to bring them back?

Scratching Up The Scenery in Shakespeare

A 1990 adaptation of the Shakespeare classic *Romeo and Juliet* featured an all-feline cast of over one hundred furry thespians! Well, all but one—the human actor, John Hurt, who played an old Italian bag lady. Physical copies of this obscure film are sparse, making it harder to find than a kitty in a field full of haystacks. Once again, it's time for action. Would anyone like to campaign to bring this furry sensation to Netflix...?

TV Nation

In 1927, all-electronic television (other less viable versions had been mechanically based) was successfully demonstrated for the first time by an American inventor Philo Farnsworth. And what was the first still image broadcast across the nation? That's right, a cat! None other than Felix the cat, the erstwhile star of the big screen, then America's most instantly recognizable star.

Television would make a wide impact on not just America but on the whole world, broadcasting entertainment and information electronically across the entire world. This was a ground-breaking development that would shape modern life like few other technologies. A new form of art and leisure was created, plus it ushered in millions of new jobs for actors, technicians, and a whole host of others. It also offered advertising agencies the opportunity to reach people in their homes in a more influential and intimate manner than ever before.

Television's new pride of place in the American home led to innovations like the T.V. dinner, a fast and convenient frozen food that allowed less time spent in the kitchen and more time relaxing with family watching favorite programs, with your comfortable cat next to the box, enjoying the warmth of the television. Remember how toasty those bulky old TV sets would get? Kitties just loved them!

The 60s and 70s were the halcyon years of the cartoon cat. *Courageous Cat and Minute Mouse* was created in 1960 by Bob Kane, who also created the TV version of Batman. Courageous had his own Cat signal, a Catmobile, and, you guessed it, a Cat Cave. The next year, *Top Cat* would air on the Saturday morning cartoons, featuring a Manhattan gang of alley cats. *The Secret Lives of Waldo Kitty* of 1975 explored the multiple hero identities of one curious kitty. I bet you sometimes wonder what fantasies of daring adventures your kitty is living out when he gets that dreamy, faraway look on his face…

Do you recall the roaring lion at the start of MGM films? Enamored of this powerful mascot and wanting to pay tribute to it, producer and actress Mary Tyler Moore was determined to have an even cuter and much *tinier* mascot for her Mary Tyler Moore Productions. The MTM crew carefully followed a litter of newborn kittens belonging to one of their film editors, hoping for a toothy snarl or growl, but what they ended up with was little Mimsy, the orange tabby, and her delicate yawn. It was the perfect counterpoint for Leo the Lion's roar. Mimsy's mew would open several MTM programs from 1968 through 1988 before the concept was continued with several other cat actors.

The 1980s saw the dawn of a quite post-modern TV concept… Of course, I'm speaking of none other than *Itchy & Scratchy*, the cartoon cat and mouse series that existed within another cartoon show, *The Simpsons*. Debuting in 1989, *The Simpsons* has been the longest-running animated series in America. Throughout the series, the main show has featured multiple pet cats, all named Snowball. Since the show ran for so long, it only made sense for the Simpsons family to go through so many pet cats.

Cartoon kitties aside, felines also made their mark in live-action television, as with Salem in *Sabrina the Teenage Witch*. This goofy hit show ran from the late 1990s to the early 2000s. While most of the talking cat parts were done by an animatronic cat, Salem's stunt doubles were the real live kitties Elvis, Witch, and Warlock. Talk about blurring the lines between reality and artifice.

Speaking of blurring the lines of perception and making the everyday extraordinary, the biggest TV success of recent decades has been the rise of reality TV. Just so feline TV fans wouldn't feel left out of the whole reality TV phenomenon, in 2006, the Animal Planet network debuted *Meow Mix House*, which was a series modeled after the people-focused reality show, *The Real World*. Ten cats from animal shelters across the country shared one swanky New York City apartment, competing for an executive-level position at the Meow Mix cat food company. Every week, one feline would be voted out of the competition, leaving with a year's supply of Meow Mix and an unlimited supply of love and cuddles from their newly adopted families. A panel of professional judges decided which kitty would receive the title of Meow Mix's "Feline Vice President of Research." Now, doesn't that sound like a tasty proposition no kitty could refuse?

Music and the Purr-Forming Arts

Hitting the Right Note

Have you ever listened to the sounds of your kitty purring or mewing for milk and felt that it was simply melodious to your ears? Well, that's not the only musical pleasure our felines can offer us… Cats have had a great place in music and the *purr-forming* arts! In fact, a study done by Dr. Richard Zeliony found that the hearing of our kitties is so remarkable that they can differentiate the finest subtlest variations in musical tones.

Dr. Zeliony trained cats to respond to a whistle pitched at exactly middle C, a feat very few humans could match. The cats were so on point that they did not respond to a whistle as close as just a half step off from middle C. Call Simon Cowell and tell him to get these cats as judges on American Idol. They certainly know their stuff!

All That Jazz

It's no secret what an affinity jazz musicians have for all things feline. The fact that these musicians and lovers of jazz even call themselves "cats" should be proof enough of their love. Many notable jazz cats had their own feline friends. The cover of Bill Hardman's 1978 vinyl *Home* featured him, his trusty trumpet, and a comfy black kitty settled together on the couch.

Many jazz musicians would incorporate felines into their lyrics. The number of jazz songs with cat references is remarkable, from Zen Confrey's "Kitten on the Keys" to King Oliver's "Tom Cat." King Oliver actually played his cornet on stage alongside a dozing purr-meister at Harlem's famed Apollo Theater. It really does seem like a cat can fall asleep anywhere, even with an audience!

Rockin' It

It's not surprising that cats and rock n' roll would go together. Cats like to roll around and run with crazy rockin' energy! Both rockers and cats are known for being the rebellious type. You can't tell a cat what to do, and the same goes for a rocker. With songs like "Nashville Cats" by The Lovin' Spoonful and "Cat on Tin Roof" by Blonde Redhead, the amount of kit-spiration is endless!

One notable feline rocker went by the name of Henrietta. She held a unique place at the heart of the 1960s New York City music scene. Whether she was gigging with her owner/stage manager David Tepper and his band, The Roaring Cats, or stealing Chuck Berry's watch, you never knew what this crazy kitty would get into next. Crowds loved whenever the band played at the CGBG music club alongside rock legends Jimi Hendrix and Cream. They always cheered on Henrietta the cat's spunky stage performance. Tepper once noted, "She jumped from my head to the drums and landed on top of Buddy Rich!"

Another cat lover of the sixties was John Lennon of the Beatles. This British native first came to New York in 1964 to debut on the Ed Sullivan Show for over seventy million viewers. That's around the same number of cats in America today! With a fondness for the American rock n' roll scene, he would become a permanent US resident in the 1970s, despite constant threats of deportation by the Nixon administration. Of course, efforts would fail to move this rock star or any of his *purr*-sistant cats away. That's right; he had quite a few felines guarding him...

While Lennon tried his hardest not to have a cat due to the amount of touring he did, he finally relented. He and his assistant, May Pang, would care for a black cat and a white cat whom they named Major and Minor, after the musical keys. Throughout his life, Lennon would be known as "the crazy cat lady," with over sixteen different kitties in his care. They bore noteworthy names such as Salt, Pepper, Elvis, and Jesus. I would imagine Jesus must have been a larger cat. After all, to paraphrase John Lennon's audacious appraisal of the Beatle's fame, "who's bigger than Jesus?"

Iggy Pop, "The Godfather of Punk," has a soft side, too—softer than a kitten's belly, we'd say. While shooting his film *Blood Orange*, a little gray and white stray cat pops up and takes a liking to the rockstar, following him around and laying in his lap between takes. One day, the kitten appeared quite ill, and against the cost- and deadline-focused producer's wishes, Iggy stopped filming to bring the little mite to the vet. It turned out that the poor thing had three broken ribs (possibly from a catfight, the vet said) and was on the verge of death. Iggy saved this stray's life and adopted him, naming him simply, and oh so appropriately, "Pop."

Hip Hop Cats

Hip Hop originated in The Bronx during the late 1970s. Since then, it has gone on to dominate the music scene around the world. One rapper who certainly has cats on his mind is Sterling "TrapKing" Davis, also known by the distinguished moniker of "The Cat Rapper." TrapKing would spend time between gigs working at a local shelter, mainly assisting in their TNR Program (Trap-N-Release), to catch feral cats for spay or neuter before releasing them back to the streets. Eventually, the day came when the rapper finally realized where his heart lay and left the hip hop world to start his own rescue organization called "TrapKing Humane Cat Solutions." TrapKing has worked with organizations such as the Boys and Girls Club of America to help kitties get adopted.

In 2015, Atlanta rapper Killer Mike and Brooklyn's El-P created *Meow the Jewels*, a remix of their album *Run the Jewels*, in which all the instrumentals were replaced by the sounds of cats meowing. The Kickstarter campaign amassed over $60,000 in donations for the creation of the album, all of which were donated to charity. We've got to say the amount of feline-related advocacy and philanthropy in the hip hop world is paws-down simply fur-nominal!

Down-Home Country Critters

American country music has long spoken eloquently of life's more complicated dilemmas, with some songs containing a whole novel's worth of heartbreak and confusion. The chart-topping 1966 song called "Walkin' My Cat Named Dog" by Norma Tanega tells of one such dilemma. The lyrics explain how the folk singer always wanted a dog, but that a cat was a more sensible choice due to the musician's unpredictable schedule. However, she still yearned for some canine company. Her solution was to train her cat (whom she named "Dog") to walk on a leash so she could pretend to be having some dog-style quality time. We hope that she eventually came to love her second-choice cat as much as she would have any dog. We wonder if the underappreciated cat ever wrote a country classic about playing second fiddle to a canine...

Country musicians' complicated relationships with cats continue with George Strait's 1991 song "You Know Me Better Than That." In it, he sang about how his new lover tells all her friends "that I'm perfect, and that I love her cat." That's what elevates a man to the realm of perfect? Being a cat lover should be the bare minimum! The song then goes on to say, "But you know me better than that." Excuse me? Is this man really lying about being a cat lover just to get a date? For shame! I'm sure the cat sees right through him, by the way.

The Lights Shine Bright On Broadway

The Broadway mew-sical *CATS* hit the stage in New York City in 1982. It was at that magical moment that all the kitties in the streets became just a tad more fabulous than they already were. Based on the 1939 poetry collection *Old Possum's Book of Practical Cats* by St. Louis born T.S. Eliot, the musical tells the story of a tribe of cats who must decide which kitty gets to start over and return to Earth as a fresh-eyed, bushy-tailed kitten. Ah, we see, so this must be how a cat's nine lives are determined...

An iconic song from the musical, called *Memory*, contains the lyrics, "All alone with the memory of my days in the sun, if you touch me, you'll understand what happiness is." Yes, that's right, cat lovers stroking their cats and sharing their joint memories of sunny days certainly seems like bliss to us. Over 150 notable singers have recorded their version of the kitty homage, including Judy Collins, Barry Manilow, and Barbara Streisand to name a few.

Still, not every notable feline performance piece goes on to worldwide fame, even if it was truly outstanding. A remarkable 1986 cat concert at Alice Tully Hall in New York City featured six feline soloists, who competed for a chance to win the Magical Musical Meow-Off sponsored by the pet food giant Purina. Yes, these were real kitties, not humans dressed like them! They were accompanied by a full orchestra and two human backup singers as they mewed to their heart's desire.

The winner was an orange Persian mix named Pumpkin, who was awarded $25,000 and an acting slot in one of Purina's cat food commercials. It looks like you might need to stop reprimanding your howler for practicing her singing in the middle of the night and go get her a talent scout instead!

The program for the evening also featured a *cat-tata* called "The Meow That Saved the Kingdom," which told the story of a cat kingdom under a dark spell that could only be broken with a mew-sical of meows! Now that's the kind of entertainment we can relate to…

Science

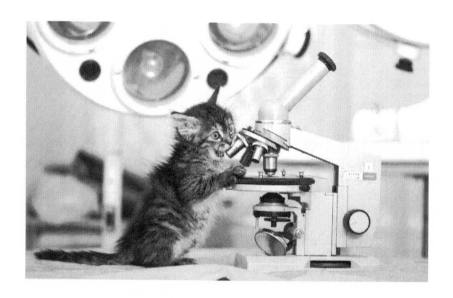

Who's A Smart Kitty?

Psychologist Dr. Maier of the University of Michigan and Dr. Schneirla at the Department of Animal Behavior in the Museum of Natural History directly compared the IQs of canines and felines based on their memory function. They showed both species a large series of boxes, introducing a dish of food found only beneath boxes that had a lighted lamp on top of them. The animals were trained to find these boxes, then kept away from them for a period of time to test their memory. They should have let some cats I know take part in this test. They would never forget where the food is hidden. Never.

The dogs were able to remember which boxes contained food for up to five minutes. Cats, however, retained this memory for up to *sixteen hours*. This discovery meant that cats had a degree of memory recollection previously thought to only belong to primates. Intelligence is defined as the ability to acquire information, retain it, and utilize it to solve problems. Given these criteria, it's safe to say that our feline friends are fairly intelligent. The next time you need to put your thinking cap on, perhaps you should consult your thinking *cat* instead.

Going Nuclear

Cats often end up where they're not supposed to be, even sneaking into a high-security nuclear power plant! The Southern California nuclear power plant, San Onofre, had heavy security consisting of barbed wire fences, metal detectors, and armed guards. Yet, in 1966 a crafty cat somehow managed to break in and have a litter of all-black kittens. Maybe what the power plant needed to add to their security were infrared cameras to spot those dark little furry shadows moving about.

When these kitties were finally found near defunct Unit 1 after about three weeks, employees carried them through the portal contamination monitors, which immediately sounded an alarm, indicating that the kitties had acquired high levels of radiation. A thorough bath lowered these levels significantly, and the babies were brought to a special facility to further remove any internal radiation as well. The kitties were affectionately named Alpha, Z beta, Gamma, and Neutron, and after seven months, they were pronounced radiation-free.

Their mother was never found; however, one employee reported finding a listless cat around the same time the kittens were found. Fortunately, testing on his clothing found very low traces of radiation, despite having held the cat closely.

Apparently, despite all the security, cats sneaking into the plant was certainly not just a one or two-time occurrence. For instance, ten years before, an employee reportedly set off contamination alarms after petting a stray. Where have these cats gone? Are they waiting underground with mew-tant kitty powers ready to take over the world? Stranger things have been known to happen.

CopyCat

On December 22, 2001, the first cloned pet was born in a lab at the Texas Agricultural and Mechanical University School of Veterinary Medicine under the direction of Dr. Westhusin and Dr. Shin. CC, short for CopyCat, was a part brown tabby and part domestic shorthair and was the only survivor of eighty-seven cloned embryos.

Scientists borrowed the DNA from her feline genetic donor,

Rainbow, a calico shorthair, and transferred it into an egg that had its DNA removed. Allie, a brown tabby, served as the surrogate mother who carried the egg through to birth. While CC had the exact genetic makeup to be a clone of Rainbow, her coat had a mix of the two cats and was not a duplicate of the cloned cat. Additionally, CC would also grow up to have a personality quite different than the cat, from whose genetic material she was cloned. Basically, in case you're thinking of making a genetic copy of your kitty, although they might be genetically the same, the clone might look differently and act differently from the original cat. It makes me wonder what the point of whole thing is, from a pet owner's perspective that is.

CC was taken home by one of the scientists on the team, Dr. Kraemer, and grew up in a normal and loving home away from a sterile laboratory environment. She passed away from old age after eighteen years of life, a fulfilling life in which she had a handsome partner named Smokey and her own natural litter of four cuddly babies. As long as there was also wet food in the equation, it sounds like CC had everything a cat could ask for!

Not long after CC, a few cats would be cloned commercially by owners who missed their deceased pets. Due to the high price paid ($50,000 in some instances), commercialized cloning was denounced by the Humane Society, arguing that the funding received for cloning could have been better used to address the growing population of homeless animals.

Feline Adventurers

In The Navy!

Throughout history, different cultures across the globe have been quick to realize how crucial kitties are to rodent control. The US Navy was no exception. In addition to their skills at pest catching, cats were thought to bring good luck. It also didn't hurt that they were darn good company on those long, lonely sea voyages. Navy crew became very attached to their kitties. There are quite a few accounts of how much they became part of life on board the ship, integrating themselves into daily routines and even witnessing some rather intense military action.

One such feline was a spotted kitty named Pooli, short for Princess Papule. She was born in 1944 in the Navy Yard at Pearl Harbor and was taken onto the attack vessel *USS*. She saw action in the Philippines, the Marianas, the Palau Group, and Iwo Jima. At the height of the action, Pooli was usually seen headed straight for the mailroom to curl up on top of a large sack of letters. We're sure this can't be attributed to cowardice. After all, someone needed to protect the confidential military intelligence doubtless contained in all that correspondence!

Pooli's birthday was celebrated fifteen years later on Independence Day 1959. The occasion was recorded in the *LA Times* newspaper. By this stage, the feline WWII veteran was blind with only her front teeth left, spending most of her days sleeping, a much-deserved rest, and a chance to dream of her thrilling naval adventures.

Is It a Bird? Is It a Plane? Darn, It's a Cat!

Amongst the bustling of busy human feet running past one another, trying to catch their flight before it took off, the tiny black paws of a small kitten pitter-pattered through the airport. He was so small and so dark, he made it through security without being spotted. To be fair, the year was 1929, just a few years after the first airports were built in America, so security wasn't exactly the highest at that point.

This stray kitten, who would later be named Blackie, even snuck onto an airplane and took a flight from California to New York, all the way on the other side of the country. While I'm sure the stewardesses weren't equipped with any complimentary cat treats, I hope they at least offered him some milk. It is a long flight after all! It seems Blackie would be the first cat to ever fly on a plane in this country, but he wouldn't be the last. Nowadays, cats don't have to fly on the down-low. If you're on an approved airline, your kitty can fly as your personal item beneath the chair or even in the seat next to you. That is, if you've paid for the extra seat, of course. Still, who could deny their furry darling that privilege? Don't blame us if your kitty complains about the airplane food. You know how picky some cats can be…

Cats in Space

Have you ever thought about living in space? How do you think your kitty would fare? I imagine it might be difficult to use a litter box in zero gravity. The folks over at NASA had some questions of their own and decided to conduct a few experiments to see how our furry critters would manage.

In 1947, the U.S. Airforce Aerospace prepared astronauts for space flight by transporting them in an aircraft cheekily called The Vomit Comet at an altitude high enough to create microgravity. Predictably, many of the trainees experienced nausea as they attempted to maneuver themselves around their new, weightless environment. Cats were brought into the aircraft and held upside down before dropping them to see how their bodies would adapt so they would manage to land on their feet. The experiment was conducted to help humans learn from the cats' movements.

Aside from providing a laugh for those rewatching the film footage, the experiment provided some useful insights. For instance, the 1962 report from the same lab that conducted the 1947 experiments, "Self Rotation Techniques for Humans in Weightless Environments," featured The Cat Reflex. A series of photos showed an astronaut side by side with a cat, contorting his body in similar ways to the feline's movements to help him turn from upside-down to right-side-up. I've always said that cats have so much to teach us, whether here on good ole planet Earth or way up near the stars.

Art and Adornment

Home Decor

The Kit-Cat Klock, a distinctive black plastic cat with sharp rolling eyes, a large smile, and an analog clock taking up the feline's rotound belly, swept the nation during the post-Depression era, cheering folks on with its quirky appearance. Its long, black tail with a white tip would swing from side to side with every tick of the second hand. The 1970s saw a resurgence of popularity for this clock, a trend that continues to the present with the release of new colors and designs, like a striking pink kitty with a pearl necklace or a bright orange and black tiger-striped kat with a snazzy bow tie! Cats have such innate style, don't they?

Elsewhere in the world of cat interiors, the first cat climbing tree was created in 1968 by Frank Crow to "provide a clawing surface with maximum appeal to cats," as well as fulfil their needs for climbing, playing, feeding, and sleeping. The first version was somewhat modest, featuring simply two scratching posts and a soft hammock at the top for restful kitty slumber. When testers asked for more places to climb, play, and to be one's best cat self, the manufacturer came up with a more sophisticated model, featuring four surface levels, five scratching posts, a large and dark slumber cave, and a rope toy at the top as a reward for the most skilled climbers. Things only got more elaborate from there. Cat habitats continue to grow in size and complexity. More ramps! Cooler toys! Later iterations would include another hideaway here, hammock swings there, getting wider and taller, with levels expanding to the heavens—a cat's proper place, whence it can look down upon us. Just like American skyscrapers, there's no stopping them. Aways bigger and better… Knock out a wall and create a glass bubble for the cat to bird watch? Done. Install a transit system along the ceiling to help our fluffballs run around the house with no obstacles? Of course! Create a custom tower that *actually* looks like a tree, complete with leaves and a trunk…Soon we will find ourselves looking for houses with enough square footage to contain these fantastical feline structures. When it comes to our kitties, we cat lovers know no limits.

Strutting Those Feline Fashions

After fighting in the American Revolutionary War, James Potter Collins became an apprentice at a tailoring shop. His memoirs recollect one Christmas night when he was left alone minding the place… *"There was nothing left me in charge to do, only to take care of the house. There was a large cat that generally lay about the fire. In order to try my mechanical powers, I concluded to make a suit of clothing for puss, and for my purpose gathered some scraps of cloth that lay about the shop-board, and went to work as hard as I could."*

He surely did complete the suit, but as he was fitting the large cat into it, the kitty happened to slip into a hole in the floorboards beneath them and didn't come back out… That is, until after the holidays when Collins's mentor and his family had returned. They were all sitting around the fireplace when the cat strutted in front of the assembled company… in his fine-tailored suit. Horrified, Collins feared his master's reprimands, but presumably the boss didn't mind too much as the suit came to be displayed in the shop's front window for all to admire.

By the 1900s, photographs of our four-legged friends dressed up in farm clothes or wedding attire started popping up from photographers like Harry Whittier. What started out as a few eccentrics dressing up their cats would later lead to a booming market for pet apparel. Fast forward to the present day. We're talking big business here. In fact, about 70% of households in America own cats, and many of those are highly likely to purchase cat-related clothes. According to *Forbes* magazine, 60% of millennials say they like to buy fashion for their pets. The aptly named Meow-Wear is one of many fashion lines for felines that create patterned carriers, sweaters, collars, and more for kitties. It's not just felines who are getting fashionable, it's also their owners who are donning cat-themed garments. That's why high-fashion designers like Ralph Lauren and Marc Jacobs all love to borrow from the greatest fashion icon—the cat. In fact, for decades, our furry kitties have been the inspiration for many fashion terms, from cat-eye makeup and kitten heels to pussy bows and catwalks. It seems just about anything stylish or fun in the fashion world has a connection to cats. Spotted feline prints are no stranger to the pattern room, and even quirky box dresses with little kittens printed onto them are adored on both the runway and in retail stores across America. Whether it's a celebrity, like Ariana Grande, or an elementary school student, it seems one thing they have in common is a desire to wear a cat-eared headband! Publications, such as *Vogue* and *PUSS PUSS Magazine,* have redefined images of what a cat lady looks like, making it cool to openly express your love for felines through your fashion choices.

Sold! To the Very Rich Cat Lady in the Back...

In 2002 the Skinner Gallery of Boston held the first major art auction that exclusively featured cat-related pieces. With over 450 pieces to bid on, featuring everything from oil paintings to sculptures and jewelry, this auction was the *purr*-fect shopping spree for feline fanatics of fine art. The Cincinnati Art Galleries auctioned a 1902 Rookwood Pottery vase called *The Cat's Meow* that featured the fluffiest of white kitties hand-painted on it by the artist Edward Timothy Hurley. This vase sold for over $12,000, double its estimated value. You and I might want to hide a vase like that very securely, or for all we know, it might soon be knocked over by one of our own real-life felines, jealous that another kitty would be getting so much attention!

Lest you think the feline art scene is confined to America's East coast, in 1994, the Philip Wood Gallery opened its doors in Berkley, California, where it features an international display of artwork created *by* cats. That's right, some clever little furballs covered their dainty paws in paint and let their inner lions roar as they dominated the canvas with precise pitter-patters and significant scratches. If you're fascinated by the subject of feline aesthetics, the recollections of many fine feline artists are documented in the must-have volume *Why Cats Paint: A Theory of Feline Aesthetics* by Busch and Silver. In it, you'll learn all about the *hiss*-tory of these sensitive souls. It seems felines make such fine painters thanks to their poised ability to stand still and stare deeply at their subject, taking in everything with their sharp eyes before transferring the images onto paper, or at least, so we're told...

Literature, The Vital Feline Connection

Literature chronicles the human experience, and as our lives are so intertwined with our cats, it's no surprise that kitties feature prominently in both American literary works and in the lives of American writers themselves. *The Black Cat* was a magazine that ran from 1895 to 1923, publishing over twenty thousand copies every month. Each cover would feature a cat dressed in that issue's theme, whether it was a struggling artist or a silly court jester. Filled with short stories, the series launched the careers of several famous writers, such as Octavius Roy Cohen and Jack London. Let's not overlook other more practical *purr*-iodicals, such as the magazine *Cat Fancy*, a publication dedicated to cat care dating back to 1965 that includes a centerfold poster of a cat in each issue!

America's cats are featured in many different literary formats. For instance, felines are to be found everywhere in poetry wherein so much of a cat's spirit can be captured eloquently in just a few evocative words. Consider Emily Dickinson's "She Sights a Bird—She Chuckles" to "The Cat's Song" by Marge Piercy or the enigmatic "A Little Language" by Robert Duncan. Of course, let's not overlook those longer-form prose works that have also provided equally perceptive glimpses of cats' inner lives. In 1901, Susan Louise Patterson published *Pussy Meow*, an autobiography written from the perspective of Fluffie the cat. This book imagines how a cat might think and feel, thereby encouraging better treatment and kindness for felines, not to be taken for granted at that time. A landmark work, it is considered the *Black Beauty* of cat books. Some other intriguing reads include Paul Gallico's *The Silent Miaow*, a manual he translated from the feline language on how to exploit and dominate humans. Of course, a love for cat literature usually starts pretty early on (as does a love for cats themselves, I'd say). I'm thinking of bestselling children's books, like Wanda Gag's 1928 book *Millions of Cats* and Dr. Seuss's *Cat in the Hat* from 1957 (perhaps the two most successful cat books of all time).

Many authors would find inspiration from their own cats when creating their stories, such as Edgar Allan Poe and his feline friend named Catarina. This kindly kitty perched on the author's shoulder as he wrote and considerately provided both love and warmth as she lay on Poe's tubercular wife's body as she lay dying while shivering in a wretched hovel Poe was then too poor to heat properly. Poe poured his life into his work, and his story *The Black Cat* is one of literature's most compelling portraits of interaction between humans and a cat, even if it is marked by desperation and callousness. Although not cruel by nature, Poe had suffered enough to understand what being subjected to cruelty felt like and hence could convey it convincingly in his work.

Poe wasn't the only literary great to adore felines. Mark Twain had as many as eleven cats at one point, with some of their names being tongue-twisting monikers such as Beelzebub, Blatherskite, and Zoroaster. He gave them such names so that his young children could get used to saying difficult words! His fascination with cats dates to his youth, and the story about Peter the cat in *The Adventures of Tom Sawyer* is actually a real-life story from his childhood. An episode from Twain's later years illustrates both how much his fans adored Twain and how highly the literary giant regarded cats. In 1905 while his daughter was convalescing in a sanatorium, Twain was looking after her black cat named Bambino. One day the little mite disappeared. Three days after the kitty vanished, Twain posted an ad in the *New York American* newspaper promising an award of $5 (worth around $150 in today's money) for the missing cat. He asked that if anyone had seen "a distinguished cat" who is "large with velvety black fur," to please bring the cat to him. It did not take long for Twain to receive a long line of fans with black cats in their arms visiting his home. All of these cat-rescuers were presumably admirers of Twain's simply dying to have a chance to chat with their hero. Bambino was soon discovered in a neighbor's yard across the street, presumably unaware of (and quite possibly unbothered by) all the fuss he had caused.

There have been (and presumably will continue to be) many books relating to cats. The prolific and highly knowledgeable Grace Pond published a plentiful collection of cat books from the late 1950s through the 1980s, one of the most notable being *The Complete Cat Encyclopedia*. In the 1970s, Chicago-based Claire Necker released an array of very interesting feline literature, such as *Supernatural Cats*, *Talking Cats*, and *Science Fiction Cats*! Necker would also author the highly important *Four Centuries of Cat Books: A Bibliography, 1570-1970*, listing over two thousand books on cats. There are, of course, many ground-breaking works from modern cat experts, such as those from Angela Sayer like *The World of Cats* and *Complete Book of the Cat*.

Ranging from historical accounts to scientific studies and captivating storytelling, thousands of books exist today for cat experts, lovers, and admirers to enjoy as they fancy. Prepare yourself; there's a lot to paw through! From my personal reading list of more recently released titles, I'd recommend *Feline Philosophy: Cats and the Meaning of Life*, as well as the gorgeously illustrated *A Cat's Tale: A Journey Through Feline History*. As an adopted New Yorker, I was mesmerized by Peggy

Gavan's *The Cat Men of Gotham: Tales of Feline Friendships in Old New York*. Of course, loath as I am to blow my own trumpet, I'm going to suggest you check out my very own *The Cats of Ireland* and *The Cats of Britain*.

Hemingway, Founder of a Cat Dynasty

American novelist Ernest Hemingway, who brought an innovative, bare-bones approach to tales of struggle and adventure, not only produced exceptional work that defined a new, pared-down approach to literature but also created a whole mini-kingdom full of cats, upon whom he bestowed imaginative names. In the 1930s, the author of *The Old Man and the Sea* and *A Farewell to Arms* resided in a French Colonial-style home overlooking the island's iconic lighthouse in Key West, Florida. This home is now a museum and is a must-visit for anyone looking to learn more about the writer, and indeed about his cats.

The Hemingway Cat story began when the Nobel-Prize winning author met a sea captain named Stanley Dexter at a bar called Sloppy Joe's (a high-class joint, we're sure). After many rounds of alcohol, the captain pulled out a six-toed kitten (who was named Snow White) from his ship as a gift for Hemingway. It seems that sailors valued these polydactyl cats (also dubbed mitten cats as it looks as though they might be wearing some) as bringers of luck and thought their extra toes gave them an edge when it came to rodent control. Hemingway immediately fell in love and soon became a polydactyl aficionado, living with a whole host of cats upon whom he bestowed names that spoke to each cat's individuality, such as Clark Gable, Princess Six-Toes, Uncle Wolfer, and Christobal. He featured some of them in his stories, such as his big, loving Persian named F. Puss in *A Moveable Feast*, his black and white

Boise in *Islands in the Stream*, and others in *Cat in the Rain* and *Killer*.

To this day, as set forth in Hemingway's will, the keepers of his house continue the tradition of homing Hemingway Cats (approximately sixty of them) on the Key West property, many of whom are direct descendants of his original ship cat, Snow White.

This Crazy Modern World

The Internet Cat to Beat All Others?

A 2007 Internet image of a gray shorthair cat with the caption, "I can has cheezburger?" is credited with bringing the trend of animal memes to the mainstream. Imagine, all those cute cat pics with some *hiss*-terical text attached to them deriving from that one original post! The meme was created by Hawaiian blogger Eric Nakagawa, whose website features the world's largest collection of "lolcats" and other funny animal memes. His website is worth millions of dollars, getting over 1.5 million daily clicks from Internet users across the globe.

You may have heard of Reddit, the online forum where people can share social news, hold discussions, and rate responses, with an average of over 800,000 posts made per day. It was here that one of the greatest Internet cat sensations ever made her debut. Grumpy Cat went viral after her owner posted a photo of her seriously upset demeanor in 2012. The photo was shared rapidly among online users. Many were convinced that the photo must have been digitally altered to make the kitty look so astonishingly dismayed. However, that wasn't the case. Grumpy Cat's real name was Tardar [sic] Sauce, a cream and brown-pointed cat from Arizona. She was petite and had a peculiar face thanks to her dwarfism, which also caused her to wobble a bit as she walked. Despite this, she lived a completely normal kitty life, well, apart from the Internet fame that she generated. She has her own website and hundreds of different kinds of merchandise ranging from swimsuits to temporary tattoos and even her own fragrance line. She also has been featured in comic books, even co-starring with that other famous feline curmudgeon, the one and only Garfield! Being cantankerous seems to be the key to fame and fortune. Perhaps I should scrunch up my face in a frown more often than I already do. Or does a sour demeanor as a one-way trip to riches only work for stardom-seeking cats?

Celebrity Companions

Cats have experienced it all, from being worshipped by some cultures, to experiencing hate due to ignorant superstitions or unfortunate depictions as agents of evil in dark folktales. Their current status, while not universally good, is, on average better than in the past. While there are still some people out there who believe cats are just no good, that hasn't stopped our felines from rising in popularity across the country, even securing enviable spots in the arms of celebrities! From Katy Perry's tabby named *Kitty Purry* to *The Walking Dead*'s tough guy, Norman Reedus's cat, *Eye in the Dark*, it's clear that these guys sure do know how to set up a cat for fame, starting with the name they bestow on them.

Although not himself famous or a celebrity's pet, one poor kitty found that even geographic proximity to fame can change one's life. Taboo was a cat that belonged to a couple who lived next door to Michael Jackson. This poor little kitty was catnapped multiple times by crazed fans who hoped for a chance to meet the celebrity if they held his cat ransom, not realizing that Taboo wasn't actually Jackson's cat. One of these times, Taboo went missing for a few days, seriously worrying his owners, Helen and Dave Arthur. Fortunately, Taboo wore a collar with their phone number on it, so it didn't take long for the Arthurs to receive a call asking for Michael Jackson. Thankfully, Taboo was safely returned by the fan who had taken him two hours away to

San Diego.

Robert Downey Jr. and his wife, Susan, rescued two special cats in 2010, a gray longhair and a black cat with the names Monty and D'Artagnan. The actor has said that he would do anything for these four-legged children, and in an interview with *Men's Fitness*, he said he would even "kill for them." This goes not just for his own cats but for any that he sees being treated poorly. That's right, you shameful cat abusers, you better watch your back because Iron Man will get you!

American Instagram Stars

Not all Instagram cats are created equal. Nala Cat holds the Guinness World Record as the most popular cat on Instagram with over 4.3 million followers! This quirky gray kitten loves taking photos with her face up close and personal to the camera, showing off her cute button nose. Sam, also known as @SamHasEyebrows, has a humbler (but nonetheless impressive) following of 230,000 people. You can certainly see the humility on his face when he has his eyebrows raised, which is all the time... They are almost permanently raised. Whether he's snoozing on the grass, wearing a shark costume, or sitting in the center of a rainbow flower, he can't help but have a look of grave concern.

Even more of these online stars can be seen by searching for the #CatsofInstagram hashtag or the channel of the same name. There, you can find saber-tooth incarnates with some serious overbites, brave little paraplegic kitties riding their bicycles, or a sassy-looking hairless cat wearing a grandpa sweater. Any cat belongs on Instagram. Remember, in America, you can make it to the top. Take a gander and add pics of your own kitties using hashtags such as #cute, #catsliketheattention, or #fluffyinfluencer.

The Future of America's Cats

Keeping Americans Healthy and Sane

Dr. John Amodeo, a marriage and family therapist who focuses on intimacy and relationships, believes people like cats *purr*-cisely for the affection that they give. Even the rhythmic action of petting a kitty's soft fur focuses our attention and gives us a calming feeling, similar to what medications offer. He says that when a cat begins to purr, they are openly showing us that they trust us and accept the affection that we give. This type of vulnerability and emotional connection allows us to be mindful in the present moment, giving and receiving tender care. The doctor is on to something. Even just picturing yourself giving your fluffball a belly rub probably relaxes you.

Studies by the American Stroke Association, as well as the National Center for Health Statistics, found that cat owners were less likely to die from heart attacks than those who have never had a cat. A ten-year-long study found that the likelihood of heart attack was as much as 40% greater for those lacking kitties and 30% higher for other cardiovascular diseases. An array of studies have confirmed that the presence of cats can release oxytocin in a person's brain, noticeably lower blood pressure, and release dopamine and serotonin, which all promote immune health by relieving stress.

People often block out deep intimacy with other people out of fear of receiving too much affection. They might feel selfish to take so much or feel vulnerable and anxious at the thought of losing affection once it's accepted. With a cat, however, the stakes are lower. Both the cat and the person can openly rely on each other for emotional support, and the ease of this relationship is what makes it so strong.

Neuroeconomist, Paul Zak, makes a solid point, explaining this is why "people spend thousands of dollars on treating a pet medically rather than get a new animal." The powerful bond between us and our fluffy balls of love is a special one that is hard to put a price on.

So, the next time you're *feline* sad, try picking up a fluffy cat and giving them a good belly rub or two. I guarantee you'll both be whiskered away!

Robo Kitties...?

Jim, a resident at Lake Park, a care home for the elderly in California, lightly pets his fluffy white cat named Bingo, basking in her affectionate purrs. Cozy to the touch, you wouldn't even know that this kitty was a robot if not for a bit of mechanical rigidity at its core. Okay, maybe some careful examination of the "cat's" gaze might also give the game away... The kitty has sensors all throughout her body that allow her to react to widely varying prompts. For instance, a pet along her back will produce some purrs, while a stroke of her cheeks may prompt a sharp "Miaow!" When it gets dark, she'll yawn and nod off for a little cat nap. The residents of the home really enjoy the personal connection they can have with Bingo, bringing back memories of dear pets that they used to have.

Launched in 2015, these robo cats, called "Joy For Alls," were created by Hasbro to provide comfort and companionship, especially for therapeutic purposes. Studies show that these robo kitties are particularly beneficial to those living with dementia or Alzheimer's. From such robotic companions, patients can receive a cat's affection even if they don't possess the mental or physical ability needed to care for a living one.

Researchers at Florida Atlantic University found the use of these robo kitties to be especially useful during the COVID-19 pandemic when many elderly and hospitalized people were required to quarantine and maintain social distance from friends and families. These robo kitty owners were seen having conversations with their fluffy mechanical companions, openly sharing their feelings with them and telling stories while stroking their soft yet synthetic fur. While we're sure these fake felines serve a purpose, and it does seem like a noble venture, I think we'd all say that you can't beat the real thing.

The Facts, Ma'am, Just the Facts...

Did you know?

- A group of kittens is called a kindle, whereas old-timers (adult cats) form a clowder.

- Cats can jump up to six times their own height.

- The average lifespan of a cat is twelve to fourteen years.

- A female cat is called a *queen* or *molly*.

- The most prolific cat was Dusty, a tabby from Bonham, Texas, who gave birth to 420 kittens over her lifetime; her last litter was birthed on June 12, 1952.

- The greatest recorded number of toes on a cat was thirty-two. Mickey Mouse, who resided in California, had eight toes on each foot.

- A cat has thirty-two muscles in each ear.

- As of 2021, more than 59 million cats reside in the United States.

- Over a third of households in the United States have at least one cat.

- The state with the highest percentage of cat owners in the United States is Vermont, with about 49.5%.

- Cats are now so cherished by Americans that there is even a National Cat Day, celebrated each year on October 29th!

- A cat can make over one hundred vocal sounds (those poor old dogs can only manage ten).

⊙ Cats sleep an average of fourteen hours a day.

⊙ Americans spend more annually on cat food than on baby food.

⊙ The average cat food meal is equivalent to about five mice.

⊙ Besides smelling with their nose, cats can smell with an additional organ called the Jacobson's organ, located in the upper surface of the mouth.

Some Final Words

I'm incredibly interested in people's stories, what they do, and why they do it. I'm also endlessly fascinated by America, a vast, ever-evolving land full of possibilities that offers people so many different paths they can follow. I've just shared some stories of Americans and the paths they took and the cats that made their journey so much more pleasant—and interesting—along the way. And let there be no doubt about it, cats will continue to play a crucial part in American life. As the American Association of Feline Practitioners has stated, cats are the most popular pets in America because they make the best companions for people who live alone or work for very long hours. When you've had a grueling day (who doesn't nowadays?), and you finally make it back home, there is no better feeling than kicking off your shoes and watching your furry little kitty pitter-patter toward you. There is always warmth and affection in a home that houses a cat. Whether they are admired for their independence, playfulness, sweet charm, or quirky antics, we all have different reasons for loving cats so dearly. In twenty-first-century America, while we don't necessarily need them as mousers as much as we used to, we've managed to make them a central part of our lives as counselors and companions, a position I see them occupying furr-ever and ever...

About The Author

Originally from Ireland, I'm a writer, editor, and researcher based in New York. I'm always on the lookout for interesting and unusual books, mainly about less obvious takes on already well-documented topics.

As you might imagine, I have a great interest in quirky "hey, how about that?" stories that make you smile, whether those tales are from history or the present day. Bearing all this in mind, off I set in search of an easy-to-read, funny little book about the role cats have played in American society. So many of us own cats and America is such a fascinating country, I thought there must be something out there. So, off I set... There were heart-warming and hilarious books about specific American cats, satirical books that featured cats, books about cats in world history, books about important people and their cats, but I couldn't find a book about American cats that might tell how they wove their way American society and the hearts of its citizens.

Well, like many of you, if I can't find what I'm looking for in a store, I'll have a shot at making it myself! I had already written a book about "The Cats of Ireland," so I reckoned "The Cats of America" might not take too long. Boy, was I wrong! The more I researched, the more I found... Pioneers and their cats, cats who were thieves, cats who were heroes, cats who inspired high fashion. Was there no end to America's felines and their far-reaching impact on American culture? Honestly, there was enough out there for an encyclopedia. However, I'm happy to leave the writing of scholarly, in-depth analyses to people who are far smarter than I am. After quite some thought, I decided to write a book of kooky stories you wouldn't believe, facts that would pique your interest, trivia that might intrigue, all told in a chatty, off-the-cuff style. Anyhow, I hope you enjoy my very personal, quite goofy collection of why I think cats are way more special than we give them credit for and why Americans love them so much. By the way, I plan to write more cat books, so if you'd like to get free advance copies of those, just go to GET YOUR FREE BOOK at the very beginning of this book. Don't say I never 'do nothing' for you! Seriously though, have fun reading this book. I'm so pleased that you've been interested enough in America and its wonderful cats to add this cheeky little volume to your bookshelf...

OTHER BOOKS BY SÉAMUS MULLARKEY...

If you enjoyed "The Cats of America," and you'd like some further feline reading material, you may wish to purr-chase "The Cats of Ireland." This tantalizing title is full of Irish cat adventures, fun facts, and cat stories galore...

DID YOU KNOW?

- There's a luxury Irish hotel that gives plain old kitties the 5-Star treatment?
- That Irish pop star Enya hides from the world in a castle by the sea--that's packed full of felines?
- That in medieval times any Irish cat was worth a whopping three times as much as a cow?

NOW YOU CAN DISCOVER...

- How you can say goodbye to the rat race and move to Ireland with your cat.
- How catnip farming could be the future for Irish agriculture.
- The very best Irish cat names for your brand-new kitten.

AND.. much, much more!

This unique book features Irish cat stories, historical Irish trivia, and fun feline facts from Ireland that are sure to *entertain* and *intrigue* you. **Purr-chase** *it on Amazon through the link below...*

https://rb.gy/yvdrbe

SPECIAL BONUS!

Want This Bonus Book for free?

Get FREE, unlimited access to it and all of my new books by joining the Fan Base!

SCAN W/ YOUR CAMERA TO JOIN!

ENJOYED THIS BOOK? PLEASE LEAVE A REVIEW...

Reviews are the most powerful tool when it comes to getting the word out about my books. I would love to be able to promote a book like the big publishing houses, but I'm just a one-man operation and can't take out full-page ads in the newspapers like they do.

However, I do have a treasured resource that these publishers would do anything to get their hands on.

A kind and loyal group of readers who aren't afraid to share the love…

Sincere, honest reviews that come from the heart bring my books to the attention of other readers, who will hopefully like them just as much.

If this book brought you a few moments of pleasure, I'd be forever grateful if you took just a few minutes out of your busy day to leave a review (don't worry if it's just a couple of words) on the book's Amazon page. You can get to the review page simply by following the link or QR code below. Thanks!

https://rb.gy/5pbrtz

PURRR-LEAZE, WON'T YOU LEAVE A REVIEW.....?

CREDITS FOR ILLUSTRATIONS

Gotta Love That American Spirit

https://image.shutterstock.com/image-photo/little-cat-chasing-mouse-600w-797302390.jpg

--Royalty-free stock photo ID: 797302390—Used under license from shutterstock.

Playing A Key Part In Our History

https://www.shutterstock.com/image-photo/skipper-cat-sailing-yacht-rigging-97736837

--Royalty-free stock photo ID: 97736837—Used under license from shutterstock

At the Heart of Our American Institutions

https://image.shutterstock.com/image-photo/portrait-furry-cat-transparent-round-600w-1240986700.jpg

--Royalty-free stock photo ID: 1240986700—Used under license from shutterstock.

Crime Don't Pay!

https://www.shutterstock.com/image-photo/cat-criminal-behind-bars-224726635

--Royalty-free stock photo ID: 224726635—Used under license from shutterstock.

A Stranger Is Just A Friend You Haven't Met

https://www.shutterstock.com/image-photo/beautiful-elegant-black-cat-lies-on-1347129014

--Royalty-free stock photo ID: 1347129014—Used under license from shutterstock.

Always On The Move

https://image.shutterstock.com/image-photo/cat-on-railway-track-600w-779633413.jpg

--Royalty-free stock photo ID: 779633413—Used under license from shutterstock.

Places and Plants With Feline Associations

https://www.shutterstock.com/image-photo/cat-grand-canyon-1138758749

--Royalty-free stock photo ID: 1138758749—Used under license from shutterstock.

Athletic Accomplishments

https://www.shutterstock.com/image-photo/kitten-ball-238701115

--Royalty-free stock photo ID: 238701115—Used under license from shutterstock.

Feline Folklore

https://www.shutterstock.com/image-photo/silhouette-spooky-black-cat-halloween-creepy-1147779443

--Royalty-free stock photo ID: 1147779443—Used under license from shutterstock.

Séamus Mullarkey

Some Notable Cats (and Some Pretty Cool Humans)

https://www.shutterstock.com/image-photo/portrait-young-women-cat-698624245

--Royalty-free stock photo ID: 660107443—Used under license from shutterstock.

Boo, Hiss! Those Cat Haters

https://unsplash.com/s/photos/angry-cat

--Royalty-free photo, no attribution required, used under license from Underslpash

It Ain't What You Say, It's the Way That Ya Say It

https://www.shutterstock.com/image-photo/word-procrastination-made-cubes-next-dozing-1997617100

--Royalty-free stock photo ID: 1997617100—Used under license from shutterstock.

Strange and Spooky

https://unsplash.com/photos/_AHEpAdR8Xo

--Royalty-free image—Used under license from Unsplash

E Purr-i-bus Unum: Some Fascinating Stories of Popular Cat Breeds

https://www.pexels.com/photo/tabby-cat-on-open-book-582070/

--Royalty-free photo, by Heather McKeen from Pexels.com

Gathering Places—For Humans and Cats Alike!

https://www.shutterstock.com/image-photo/patron-sammys-bowery-follies-downtown-bar-252139459

--Royalty-free stock photo ID: 384556630—Used under license from shutterstock.

Now That's Entertainment!

https://image.shutterstock.com/image-photo/cat-on-old-camera-600w-384556630.jpg

--Royalty-free stock photo ID: 384556630—Used under license from shutterstock.

Music and the Purr-Forming Arts

https://www.shutterstock.com/image-photo/persian-cat-longhaired-breed-characterized-by-531060532

--Royalty-free stock photo ID: 531060532—Used under license from shutterstock.

Science

https://www.shutterstock.com/image-photo/little-assistant-170985962

--Royalty-free stock photo ID: 170985962—Used under license from shutterstock.

Séamus Mullarkey

Feline Adventurers

https://www.shutterstock.com/image-photo/tabby-cat-mountains-covered-snow-behind-1032080548

--Royalty-free stock photo ID: 1032080548—Used under license from shutterstock.

Art and Adornment

https://www.shutterstock.com/image-photo/sitting-cat-gold-frame-198955439

--Royalty-free stock photo ID: 198955439—Used under license from shutterstock.

Literature, The Vital Feline Connection

--Royalty-free photo, by Tucker Good on Unsplash—Used under license from Unsplash.

This Crazy Modern World

https://image.shutterstock.com/image-photo/cute-cat-glasses-smartphone-sleeping-600w-1873704619.jpg

--Royalty-free stock photo ID: 1873704619—Used under license from shutterstock.

The Future Of America's Cats

https://image.shutterstock.com/image-photo/scottish-cat-sitting-on-stand-600w-1406294093.jpg

--Royalty-free stock photo ID: 1406294093—Used under license from shutterstock.

The Facts, Ma'am, Just The Facts

https://www.shutterstock.com/image-photo/three-black-kitten-portraits-cats-identical-638467297

--Royalty-free stock photo ID: 638467297—Used under license from shutterstock.

About the Author

Photograph author's own

--Free for commercial use, no attribution required

Enjoyed this book? Please leave a review…

--Royalty-free photo—used under license from pexels, lina-kivaka-1741205

Made in the USA
Middletown, DE
13 March 2022